STUFFED

STUFFED

LUSCIOUS FILLED TREATS
FROM SAVORY TO SWEET

CHRIS FENNIMORE

st. lynn's
press

Pittsburgh

Stuffed
Luscious Filled Treats from Savory to Sweet

ISBN-13: 978-1-943366-44-6

Library of Congress Control Number: 2019933548
CIP information available upon request

First Edition, 2019

St. Lynn's Press . POB 18680 . Pittsburgh, PA 15236
412.466.0790 . www.stlynnspress.com

Book design – Holly Rosborough
Editor – Catherine Dees

Photo credits: All photos by Laura Petrillo, except for the following:
Pohaça photo courtesy of Sevil Aktas

Illustrations by Maryann Kranis

Printed in Canada
On certified FSC recycled paper using soy-based inks

This title and all of St. Lynn's Press books may be purchased for educational, business or sales promotional use. For information please write:
Special Markets Department . St. Lynn's Press . POB 18680 . Pittsburgh, PA 15236

10 9 8 7 6 5 4 3 2 1

To my mother,
Mary Ann Felice Fennimore.

In her gentle and yet determined way,
she taught her children a love of food and
the joy of sharing that love with others.

Thanks, Mom.

Table of Contents

Table of Contents *(continued)*

Introduction

Italians have their ravioli, Chinese their dumplings, and Poles their pierogi. All around the world and for generations people have enjoyed the experience of little balls of dough stuffed with a variety of fillings. It might be cheese or meat or potatoes, sauced with tomatoes, soy sauce or melted butter, but people love them.

And these are not the only "stuffed" foods that cross borders and culinary traditions. Think about empanadas, Cornish pasties and calzone. So it got me wondering why there is such a seemingly universal love of one food stuffed inside another. And I think there are a few good reasons.

First of all, when a filling is cooked inside some form of shell, the flavorings and spices are intensified and melded together in a unique way. It extracts the juices from meat and vegetables without drying them out. It brings the ooze to cheese and marries it to other filling elements.

And then there is the contrast of textures that juxtaposes flaky with creamy in one bite, or smooth with crunchy, or the rich with the mild.

Finally, the combinations create flavor pairings that transcend each individual element.

I have been fascinated with stuffed foods for years and collect them from every tradition I can find.

For the most part, these are ethnic foods, and it is curious to see the parallels in technique as well as ingredients. But it also means that these are predominantly comfort foods with long and well loved traditions. Many of the preparations are labor intensive since they involve the assembly of individual portions, if not individual bites. But the end results are delicious and deeply satisfying.

For the past twenty-five years I have been the producer and host of a series of cooking programs on public television. Unlike other cooking formats, these shows and the resulting cookbooks invited our viewers to send us their family treasures. We asked some of them to appear on the show and share their kitchen wisdom and family stories. From time to time in this book you will see recipes from some of those home cooks – recipes forged on the appetites of real people and made in home kitchens just like yours. No special ingredients or fancy equipment required. The show was called "QED Cooks" here in Pittsburgh and "America's Home Cooking" when episodes aired around the country. The rest of the recipes I've accumulated over the years from family and friends and made my own. Feel free to add and subtract where you like to make them just as much your own.

Chris

About Recipe Proportions and Equivalents

When people call or write about the recipes we prepare on the WQED cooking programs, a fair number are complaining that they are only cooking for one or two. My usual response is that you can always make the full recipe and simply freeze the remainder in one or two serving increments. But I know there are times when freezer space isn't available and you don't want to eat the same thing for six weeks in a row. So here are a few guidelines for dividing and conquering.

- **Baking is much more precise than regular cooking and the chemical reactions require more accurate measurements.**

  For this reason, many cookbooks offer amounts in weight rather than volume. This makes it pretty easy to halve or quarter.

- **Don't confuse dry measures with liquid measure with weights.**

  They all have different characteristics. One stick of butter = 8 tablespoons = ½ cup = ¼ pound. Make sure to use the proper measuring system and measuring devices.

- **Eggs are usually the least common denominator.**

  If a recipe calls for one egg and you want to cut it in half you'll either have to whisk the egg and pour off half or use the whole egg and reduce some other liquid by about a tablespoon and a half.

- **More is not always better.**

  If I like an ingredient such as nuts or garlic, I tend to use more than the recipe calls for. That's usually not a problem, but changing the proportion of butter or sugar can change the consistency and chemistry.

- **Halving a recipe will not always cut cooking time.**

  Four muffins will take almost as much time to bake as 24 but a 2-egg frittata will cook somewhat faster than a 12-egg version.

- **When you alter a recipe, take good notes.**

  If it doesn't turn out the way you want, modify the ingredients or cooking time to improve your next attempt. Too moist, too dry, too salty? Next time will be better.

For the most part, cooking is a very forgiving science, so use the recipes as guidelines until you've perfected a version that suits your needs and tastes.

PART ONE

DOUGH

The concept couldn't be simpler. Take some dough, any dough, wrap it around a tasty morsel of meat, cheese, vegetable, or any combination thereof, and then fry, bake, boil or braise it until the dough is cooked and the filling is succulent. I have a feeling this has been going on in kitchens from one end of the globe to the other for millennia.

Once I started making my own ravioli, I realized what a labor of love it was for my mother to sit for hours rolling out dough, portioning the filling, sealing and crimping. Only then did I finally get it. It is the labor and the love that make these tasty treats so much more than just something to eat. Just like the Asian families who gather around the table to make mountains of dumplings to celebrate the New Year, the value of these dishes is in the sharing.

I encourage you to try these recipes as group projects. Make an assembly line of fillers and crimpers and make batch after batch of memories that will last much longer than the recipes themselves.

Butternut Squash Ravioli

4 dinner servings or 6 first courses

Ravioli are the kind of labor intensive foods that you only want to make by hand for the people you love. My mom would make them on special occasions but we were fortunate to have several places in our neighborhood where we could buy fresh pasta. I love to make the butternut squash version in the fall when there are plenty of squash to be had at the farmers' markets. The butter/sage sauce contains the essence of fall flavor.

INGREDIENTS

DOUGH:

2 cups semolina

2 eggs

1 teaspoon salt

1 teaspoon olive oil

Water

FILLING:

One medium to small butternut squash

¼ cup mascarpone or goat cheese

¼ cup grated Parmigiano-Reggiano cheese

1 grating of nutmeg

1 teaspoon salt

½ teaspoon white pepper

SAUCE:

1 stick butter
8 sage leaves

STEPS

1. *For the dough:* Put all ingredients except the water into a food processor. Pulse until blended. Turn on and slowly add water until a dough ball forms. Remove from the processor and knead into a smooth ball. Wrap in plastic and refrigerate for 20 minutes.

2. Preheat the oven to 375 degrees F.

3. Cut the squash in half lengthwise and scrape out the seeds. Put cut side down on a piece of buttered aluminum foil on a baking pan. Bake for one hour until very soft. Allow to cool.

4. *For the filling:* Scrape out the squash and spread it on the baking sheet. Return to the oven for another 10 minutes until the pulp is drier. Remove from the oven and cool. Put the squash pulp into a food processor with the other filling ingredients and process until smooth. This should make about 2 cups of filling. Refrigerate until ready to fill the ravioli.

5. Divide the dough into 6 pieces. Take one piece at a time and coat liberally with semolina flour. Roll out into a 4-inch-wide strip using a flat rolling pin or a pasta roller. If you are using a ravioli mold, lay the first sheet over the mold. Fill each slot with about 1 tablespoon of the filling. I usually brush some water along the edges to help the ravioli seal. Cover with a second layer of dough. Use your rolling pin to gently press and seal the two layers together.

6. If you don't have a ravioli mold, you can simply lay out a strip of dough 4 x 12 inches. Place tablespoons of the filling at even intervals about 1/4 inch from the near long edge and starting about 1/4 inch from the side. Brush some water on the dough around the filling and fold the dough over. Carefully press between the mounds to seal. Cut the individual ravioli and crimp well along the three sides.

7. Gently add the ravioli to a pot of boiling water. When the water comes back to a boil, lower the heat and simmer for 2 to 3 minutes until the ravioli are floating. Meanwhile, heat the butter in a large skillet and when melted add the sage leaves. Cook gently just until the butter begins to brown. Add the cooked and drained ravioli and stir gently to coat. Serve with additional grated cheese.

Cheese Ravioli

4 dinner servings or 6 first courses

INGREDIENTS

DOUGH:

2 cups semolina

2 eggs

1 teaspoon salt

1 teaspoon olive oil

Water

FILLING:

1 pound ricotta

1 egg

½ cup grated pecorino Romano cheese

4 tablespoons chopped Italian (flat leaf) parsley

Salt and pepper

STEPS

1. *For the dough:* Put all ingredients except the water into a food processor. Pulse until blended. Turn on and slowly add water until a dough ball forms. Remove from the processor and knead into a smooth ball. Wrap in plastic and refrigerate for 20 minutes.

2. *For the filling:* Beat the ricotta cheese with the egg until well combined. Stir in the grated cheese, salt (not too much because the cheese is naturally salty) and pepper. Chop the parsley coarse or fine and fold into mixture. Refrigerate until ready to use.

3. Divide the dough into 6 pieces. Take one piece at a time and coat liberally with semolina flour. Roll out into a 4-inch-wide strip using a flat rolling pin or a pasta roller. If you are using a ravioli mold, lay the first sheet over the mold. Fill each slot with about 1 tablespoon of the filling. I usually brush some water along the edges to help the ravioli seal. Cover with a second layer of dough. Use your rolling pin to gently press and seal the two layers together.

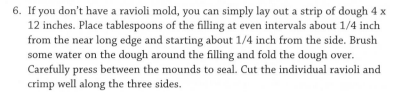

6. If you don't have a ravioli mold, you can simply lay out a strip of dough 4 x 12 inches. Place tablespoons of the filling at even intervals about 1/4 inch from the near long edge and starting about 1/4 inch from the side. Brush some water on the dough around the filling and fold the dough over. Carefully press between the mounds to seal. Cut the individual ravioli and crimp well along the three sides.

7. Gently add the ravioli to a pot of boiling water. When the water comes back to a boil, lower the heat and simmer for 2 to 3 minutes until the ravioli are floating. Drain and serve with with your favorite sauce and additional grated cheese.

Pierogi

Makes 24 to 36

There are as many spellings for these little Eastern European dumplings as there are fillings: *perogi, perogie, pierogi, pierogie, pirohi, pirohy*. Fill them with potatoes, cheese, sauerkraut, lekvar (prune or apricot butter), ground meat, mushrooms, etc. That means you can serve them as appetizers, main courses and even dessert. They are also a delicious and creative way to use leftover bits from the refrigerator mixed in with any of the above ingredients.

When we did the "E" IS FOR ETHNIC cooking marathon, Dr. James Baran came on the show to make what the children in his family used to call "poor doggies" because they misheard the name. He submitted the recipe in honor of his mother, Mary Baran.

INGREDIENTS

FILLING:

2 pounds farmer's cheese

1 egg

1 teaspoon salt

1 tablespoon sugar

DOUGH:

5 cups flour

3 eggs

1 cup plain mashed potatoes, nothing added

1 teaspoon salt

1 cup water, more or less

OPTIONAL INGREDIENTS:

Butter

Onions

STEPS

1. Mix all filling ingredients together well. Keep cold until ready to use.

2. Place flour on a large cutting board. Make a well in the center, add eggs, potatoes and salt. Mix together as for pasta. Add water 2 to 3 tablespoons at a time and knead the dough. Continue kneading until smooth and does not stick to the board. Allow to rest 5 minutes. Do not knead too much.

3. Divide the dough into 4 parts. Roll out 1 part at a time into 1/8- to 1/4-inch thickness. Cut out circles of any size you wish; a water glass works well. Place 1 tablespoon of filling on each circle and press edges together to form a half circle. Place on a floured piece of waxed paper. Bring 3 quarts of water to boil. Add pierogi and boil 3 to 5 minutes. Drain in colander.

Variations: Serve with melted butter to which 1/2 cup onions have been added. The cooked pierogies can also be fried in butter and onions until crisp. Season to taste with salt and pepper.

Pork Dumplings

Makes 24

In the era before fast food restaurants on every corner, people didn't eat out nearly as much. Trips to restaurants were reserved for special occasions. Now, it's unlikely that anyone can get from home to work without passing at least three places to get a breakfast sandwich. We don't even make our own coffee anymore! It's a wonder the supermarkets can stay in business.

I distinctly remember the first food I ate that wasn't homemade. That day, Mom hadn't started dinner as usual around 4 o'clock. She just went about her housework and when we got nervous enough to ask, she told us Dad was coming home with a surprise. He came through the door a little later than usual carrying a large paper bag from which emerged peculiar white boxes with little metal handles. The aromas were tantalizing but totally foreign. From those small containers emerged the most exotic dishes: rice that was colored brown and mixed with peas and stringy things and even bits of scrambled eggs; a gooey looking mixture

INGREDIENTS

FILLING:

½ pound fresh ground pork (you can substitute ground chicken or turkey)

3 tablespoons water chestnuts, cut in ⅛-inch dice

¼ cup scallions, finely chopped

½ teaspoon salt

1½ teaspoons sesame oil

Pinch of white pepper

1 tablespoon cornstarch

24 dumpling wrappers (these can be found in most supermarket produce sections and called wonton wrappers or skins. They come both round and square)

1 egg, beaten

2 quarts water

1 teaspoon salt

1 tablespoon peanut oil

STEPS

1. In a bowl combine the pork with the rest of the filling ingredients. Refrigerate, uncovered, at least 4 hours.

2. Put 1 tablespoon of filling in the center of each dumpling wrapper. Brush the outer edge with beaten egg and fold the round in half, crimping the edge and pushing out any air bubbles. Cook the dumplings for 5 to 7 minutes in the boiling water to which you've added salt and peanut oil. Drain and serve with dipping sauce. See recipe on page 27.

of vegetables with bits of meat and crunchy noodles for a topping; and long thin bones covered with reddish colored meat. I had my first taste of fried rice, chow mein and Chinese ribs.

On another special occasion we all jumped in the car and took the short ride to the neighborhood Chinese restaurant. At this particular place, you didn't order individual items for each person. You determined the number of people and then selected an appropriate number of dishes from lists. Six people might order four dishes; two from Column A and two from Column B. I never remember there being a Column C.

On my son's first trip to a Chinese restaurant, I was trying to pick something he would be willing to eat. In those days, his tastes were limited to chicken nuggets and pasta. We got him an order of dumplings because they seemed like the closest thing to ravioli. He loved them and still can't get enough.

Cabbage Dumplings

Makes 40 to 50

INGREDIENTS

FILLING:

2 cups finely chopped Napa or Savoy cabbage (some leaves reserved for steaming)

1 green onion, finely chopped

1 tablespoon soy sauce

1 teaspoon toasted sesame oil

1 teaspoon fresh minced garlic

1 tablespoon seasoned rice vinegar

Dash of white pepper

½ teaspoon cornstarch

40–50 dumpling wrappers

STEPS

1. Mix all the filling ingredients. Lay out 6 of the dumpling wrappers on the table and put a teaspoon of filling in the center of each. Use your finger or a pastry brush to put a thin coating of water around the edge of the wrapper. Fold the wrapper over to form a half-moon shape and pinch the edges tightly to enclose the filling. It is traditional to gather one side of the dumpling into several pleats but it's not necessary. Continue with the remaining wrappers and place the completed dumplings on a wax paper or parchment-lined tray.

2. *Two ways to cook them:* You can boil the dumplings by dropping them gently into a pot of boiling water. They will take about 10 minutes and will float to the top. But I prefer to use a steamer: Cover the bottom of your steamer with the reserved leaves of Napa or Savoy cabbage. Place the dumplings in the steamer and steam for 15 to 20 minutes. Serve with dipping sauce. See recipe on next page.

Pork and Shrimp Dumpling Filling

For 40 to 50 dumplings

INGREDIENTS

FILLING:

¼ pound ground pork

1 pound shrimp, peeled and deveined

1 green onion, chopped

1 small can water chestnuts, finely diced

1 clove garlic, minced

1 teaspoon minced fresh ginger

½ cup cilantro

1 tablespoon soy sauce

1 teaspoon toasted sesame oil

1 dash of white pepper

STEPS

1. Place all the ingredients in the bowl of a food processor. Pulse until the shrimp is finely chopped and the ingredients are well mixed. Do not over process. Proceed as with the pork dumplings to fill and steam or boil.

Note: Once you have filled the dumplings, they can be frozen on a baking sheet and then put in a plastic bag for storage in the freezer.

Dipping Sauce for Dumplings

INGREDIENTS

⅓ cup soy sauce

1 teaspoon toasted sesame oil

1 teaspoon seasoned rice vinegar

¼ teaspoon red pepper flakes (optional)

Chinese Egg Rolls

Makes 40 to 50

Contributed by
Yu Ling Cheng Behr

Yu Ling: My family is from Taiwan, a beautiful island in Asia, rich in history, culture, tech and of course, food. The Taiwanese people are very welcoming and love to share about their culture and food. In fact, family recipes are a source of pride for many Taiwanese families. Because the island is small and highly populated, multi-generations live together in the same home and that is how family history and family recipes are passed down.

I learned to cook from my mother who taught me our family recipes as well as her own creations. Oftentimes, these recipes are simply taught orally in the kitchen with no written recipe. Cooking is also important in Asian culture because it brings family together for meals. Many dishes are served family style and that simple act of passing dishes and sharing deepens bonds between family and friends.

INGREDIENTS

1 head Chinese cabbage (shredded and diced)

1 carrot, grated

3 eggs

½ pound pork, thinly sliced (bite-size)

1 tablespoon soy sauce

1 tablespoon cornstarch

½ tablespoon sugar

½ pound baby shrimp

1 bunch green onions, diced

2 packages square eggroll wrap

Canola oil for deep frying (about 2 cups for a small saucepan)

Salt and pepper to taste

STEPS

1. Add a little oil in a pan and sauté cabbage and grated carrots until cabbage is wilted. You may add salt to taste. Using a slotted spatula, remove cabbage and carrot to a bowl. Be careful to drain as much liquid as possible from the cabbage (otherwise, the egg rolls will be soggy).

2. Beat 2 of the eggs and add a little salt and pepper. Heat up frying pan with a small amount of oil. Pour in egg batter and cook a thin layer of egg. Once cooked, remove to a cutting board and let cool. Once cool, thinly slice the egg and set aside.

3. In a bowl, mix pork, soy sauce, cornstarch and sugar. Then, lightly fry the pork until meat is cooked through. Set aside in bowl and let cool. Add a little oil to the pan and cook the baby shrimp. Set aside in bowl and let cool. Once all the ingredients are cool, mix the cabbage, carrots, egg and pork together.

4. Beat the last egg in a bowl. This egg will be the "glue" for the egg roll.

5. Carefully peel off an egg roll wrap. Turn it so it faces you like a diamond. Add the cabbage, carrots, egg and pork mixture in a straight horizontal line in the bottom third of the diamond. Add 2 to 3 baby shrimp and diced green onion (to taste) on top.

6. Roll the egg roll (similar to a burrito). Start with the bottom point, roll it over the inside toppings and continue rolling until halfway. Then fold the sides in and continue rolling. When you get to the top point, brush a little beaten egg to it and finish rolling. The egg mixture acts as "glue" and should hold your egg roll together. Continue making egg rolls until you run out of ingredients.

7. In a small saucepan, pour in the canola oil and turn the heat to medium-high. Carefully add 2 to 3 egg rolls into the pan and deep fry. Be sure to turn each egg roll over several times to avoid burning it. It's important not to add too many egg rolls into the pan at one time. Enjoy!

Note: Egg rolls are also very easy to freeze. After rolling them, and before deep frying, put them on a baking tray lined with parchment paper. Set in freezer for 30 to 45 minutes or until egg rolls are frozen. Then put frozen egg rolls into a freezer zip bag. Since you already pre-froze them, the egg rolls should not stick together. When you're ready to cook them, no need to thaw. Simply deep-fry them.

Egg rolls are one of my favorite foods. I love the crunchiness of the egg roll wrapper and the tasty mix of vegetables, pork and shrimp. In my opinion, it provides a well-balanced meal all in one wrapper. Sometimes I think this is how my mother convinced me to eat vegetables – by putting them inside an egg roll! I also appreciate the time I spend with my mother when we make egg rolls together. We can easily spend a day making hundreds of egg rolls. We talk and laugh as we make them. Recently, my young daughters, Catheryn and Caroline, started to help make egg rolls, so we now have three generations of women working together.

The best part about egg rolls is there is no set recipe. You can mix together the ingredients you like and make your own version. If you need a place to start, then I hope you'll try my family's egg roll recipe.

Manicotti

Makes about 15

The first time I decided to cook a meal for my friends I called my mother and asked her for the recipe for manicotti. Having made it a million times, she knew the proportions by heart: "First you beat a dozen eggs ..." I knew I was in trouble because there were only going to be four of us for dinner and Mom had no idea how to make a smaller batch of the Italian crepes. Her recipe evolved because we purchased ricotta in three-pound tins and that made enough filling for five dozen manicotti.

Here's a scaled-down version of Mom's manicotti.

INGREDIENTS

CREPES:

1 cup flour

½ cup water

½ cup milk

¼ teaspoon salt

4 eggs

FILLING:

1 pound ricotta

½ cup grated pecorino Romano cheese

1 cup shredded mozzarella

2 tablespoons fresh parsley, chopped

Salt and pepper

1 quart tomato sauce

STEPS

1. Whisk the crepe ingredients together and let rest for 1 hour. Heat an 8-inch pan over medium-high heat and coat with nonstick spray. Pour in just enough batter to cover the bottom of the pan. When the crepe is just dry, turn and cook for a few seconds more. Stack the crepes on a plate. If you are not making the manicotti immediately, you can cover the crepes with plastic wrap and store in the refrigerator for up to one day.

2. Preheat the oven to 350 degrees F.

3. Mix the filling ingredients together. Spread about 2 tablespoons of the filling across each crepe and roll up. Place seam side down in a baking dish that has a layer of tomato sauce in the bottom. Spread a little more sauce along the top and sprinkle with additional grated cheese. Cover with foil and bake for about 25 minutes.

Kreplach

Makes 24

Another feature that is shared by many cultures is that they serve certain dishes only on special occasions. It doesn't mean that you can't have Sfingi di San Giuseppe in November but you expect to have it on March 19th. And so it is with this recipe for Jewish "dumplings" called kreplach. Except that, depending on who you consult, they will tell you the dish is traditional for Rosh Hashanah, Yom Kippur, Chanukah or Purim. I just think they are delicious and appropriate for any day when a soothing bowl of chicken broth needs a little elevation.

INGREDIENTS

DOUGH:

2 cups all-purpose flour

¼ teaspoon salt

2 eggs

4–6 tablespoons cold water

FILLING:

½ pound ground beef
1 medium onion, diced fine
¼ teaspoon allspice
Salt and pepper

2 quarts chicken stock

STEPS

1. Add the flour and salt to a food processor. Pulse a few times to distribute the salt. Add the eggs and pulse until a coarse dough is formed. Add the water 1 tablespoon at a time until a smooth dough is formed and cleans the sides of the processor. Remove and knead for a few minutes on a floured board until the dough is smooth and pliable. Cover in plastic wrap and let rest at least 20 minutes.

2. *For the filling:* In a small fry pan, brown the meat over medium heat, breaking the meat up with the back of a spoon. When the meat is no longer pink, add the onions and continue to sauté until the onions are very soft. Add the allspice, salt and pepper to taste and let the mixture cool.

3. Divide the dough in half. Roll out one piece on a floured board into a large, very thin square. Cut the square into 12 squares. Put a spoon of the filling on each square then fold in half to form a triangle. Crimp the edges tightly. Repeat with the other squares and then with the second piece of dough. You should have 24 kreplach.

4. Bring the chicken stock to a simmer and drop in the kreplach. They should be tender in 15 to 20 minutes. Serve 3 to 4 noodles in a bowl with the chicken stock.

Vegetarian option: You can make a cheese filling for the kreplach by sauteing the onions in a little butter until they are soft and then adding 1½ cups of dry farmer's cheese.

Cheese Blintz

Makes 12

One of the benefits of growing up in Brooklyn was the incredible diversity of authentic cuisines. A quick ride on the subway brought you to the triumvirate of Chinatown, Little Italy and the Lower East Side. I was fascinated by the different flavors, textures and aromas coming out of these restaurant kitchens. At the Jewish deli, I feasted on potato knish, pastrami, crisp dill pickles, matzah ball soup, and this decadent dish which looks and tastes like dessert but is often eaten for breakfast or lunch.

INGREDIENTS

CREPES:

4 large eggs

1 cup flour

⅓ cup sugar

¾ cup milk

¼ cup water

1 teaspoon vanilla

FILLING:

1 cup ricotta cheese, drained

8 ounces cream cheese

¼ cup sugar

1 large egg yolk

2 teaspoons fresh lemon juice

1 teaspoon vanilla

Pinch of salt

Butter

Preserves

Sour cream

STEPS

1. *For the crepes:* Beat the eggs well and stir in the flour. Add the sugar, milk, water and vanilla and beat until well blended and smooth. Let rest for at least an hour.

2. Heat an 8-inch non-stick skillet over medium-high heat. Drizzle in a little oil or a very small pat of butter and rub out with a paper towel. Pour in just enough batter to cover the bottom of the pan and swirl the pan to make an even crepe. Cook until the top is dry and the bottom is a light golden brown. Flip and cook for another 10 seconds on the second side. Remove from the pan and stack on a flat plate. Rub out the pan with the paper towel again and repeat until all the batter is used.

3. *For the filling:* Combine all the filling ingredients and mix until smooth. Place a crepe on your work surface and spoon a tablespoon or two of the cheese filling along the near edge. Fold in the sides and roll up to encase the filling and form the blintz.

4. Melt a little butter in a skillet and place the blinzes seam side down in a single layer. Cook until light brown and then turn over and brown on the second side. Serve with sour cream and preserves.

My Mum's Stuffed Shells

6 to 8 servings

Contributed by
Maryanne Fello

*When a person's name
is associated with a dish,
that recipe becomes a
remembrance and a legacy.
Our friend Maryanne never
shows up to a potluck or
gathering of family and friends
without a huge baking dish
filled with these luscious
stuffed shells. The dish is not
complicated but the recipe
is about so much more than
ingredients and directions.
Many thanks to Maryanne for
her willingness to share this
and all the wonderful memories
contained within.*

INGREDIENTS

**1 box (12 ounces)
jumbo shells**

FILLING:

**5 cups ricotta
(46-ounce container)**

**2 cups shredded
mozzarella**

**¾ cup chopped fresh
flat leaf parsley, or
⅓ cup dried parsley**

2 eggs

2 teaspoons salt

1 teaspoon pepper

Optional: **Cooked and
drained spinach can be
added to filling.**

**6 cups of your favorite
tomato sauce (with or
without meat)**

STEPS

1. Preheat the oven to 350 degrees F.

2. Boil shells al dente. Drain. Set aside to cool on tea towel.

3. *For the filling:* In large mixing bowl combine ricotta, mozzarella, parsley, eggs, salt and pepper. Mix well.

4. Cover bottom of large baking dish with sauce. Use a heaping teaspoon of filling to stuff each shell (being careful to drain any remaining water). Place shells in rows until pan is full – do not crowd. Cover center of each row of shells with sauce. Cover with foil and bake for 30 minutes. Allow to "rest" before serving. Easy and quick.

Samosas

Makes 36

Contributed by
Arthi Subramaniam

Arthi: Samosas cross all kinds of boundaries. In India, they show up at dinner parties dressed up and dainty on porcelain plates as starters and at the same time are ubiquitous at roadside chaat (snack) stands, where they are served on paper plates. They are a favorite among students returning from school as they are with office-goers of all ages who would have a samosa as a midday snack with masala chai or coffee. The triangular pastries are typically vegetarian, as they are filled with potatoes and green peas, but they also can be packed with ground chicken or lamb.

Every summer, when my twin and I would visit my great-grandfather in Bombay (now called Mumbai) he would take us to the beach and indulge us with our favorite street foods.

(continued on page 40)

INGREDIENTS

DOUGH:

3 cups all-purpose flour

¼ cup rice flour

1 teaspoon salt

¼ cup plus 3 tablespoons canola oil

1 cup water plus
1 tablespoon, at room temperature

FILLING:

1 tablespoon canola oil

1 medium yellow or white onion, finely chopped

1 serrano chili, finely chopped

1 teaspoon turmeric powder

1 teaspoon crushed fennel seeds

½ teaspoon ground cumin

½ teaspoon ground coriander

¼ teaspoon ground cinnamon

¼ teaspoon garam masala

½ cup frozen peas, thawed

Salt to taste

2 russet potatoes, cut into quarters, boiled with skin on and then peeled (should have some texture)

2 tablespoons fresh cilantro, finely chopped

1 tablespoon fresh lemon juice

Canola oil for frying samosas

(continued on page 40)

Samosas *(continued)*

*Samosa chaat (lightly crushed
samosas topped with spiced
chickpeas, fried vermicelli,
green and tamarind chutneys
and yogurt) and freshly
squeezed sugarcane juice
redolent with ginger were
always on top of that list.*

*Homemade samosas were a
rare treat when I was growing
up in southern India because
for one we could always buy
it from the snack shop around
the corner. Secondly, making
them meant that my mother
had to spend hours in the
kitchen because no one in my
family would stop at one or two
or three.*

*My siblings and I would swoop
down on them at tiffin (a light
meal in the afternoon) and keep
asking for more like there was
no tomorrow.*

STEPS

1. In a large bowl, add all-purpose flour, rice flour and salt and mix with fingers.

2. Add oil gradually and mix dough with hand until flour mixture becomes slightly crumbly.

3. Add water gradually and knead dough with hand for at least 10 minutes until it is smooth. If dough is hard, add a little more oil. Cover with plastic wrap and set aside for at least 30 minutes.

4. *For the filling:* In a sauté pan, warm oil over medium heat. Add onion and chili and cook until onion is slightly opaque and soft. Add turmeric, fennel, cumin, coriander, cinnamon and garam masala, and cook for 2 minutes. Add peas and cook for 2 minutes. Turn off flame, add salt and mix well. Remove pan from fire. Crumble boiled and peeled potatoes with hands and add to onion. Add cilantro and lemon juice and mix well. Set aside filling to cool.

To assemble:

1. Divide dough into 18 balls and cover with a damp kitchen towel or plastic wrap. With rolling pin, roll out each ball into 6-inch circle without using any extra flour. Then, using a pizza cutter or knife, divide the circle exactly in half to make 2 semicircles.

2. Fold 1 semicircle to create a cone by taking one edge and placing it to the other edge. Dip finger in water and moisten edges of round sides and gently press the sides together to seal them.

3. Stuff cone with potato-pea filling, making sure to push it down. Wet finger again and moisten the open inside edges of cone and press to seal them together. Make sure all the edges are sealed well; otherwise the filling will spill out when the samosa is fried.

4. Place samosa on a big plate and cover with a plastic wrap. Repeat steps for remaining semicircles. As you get to the 20th samosa, heat oil in a wok or 3-quart saucepan. Once oil is hot, fry samosas until they are golden brown.

5. Serve hot with fresh cilantro chutney and/or tamarind chutney.

Cilantro Chutney

INGREDIENTS

2 cups cilantro, including leaves and stalks, coarsely chopped

½ cup mint leaves

½ serrano chili, chopped

1 tablespoon fresh lemon juice

1 teaspoon salt

½ teaspoon ground cumin

STEPS

1. Blend all ingredients with a little water to a smooth chutney.

Tamarind Chutney

INGREDIENTS

4 teaspoons tamarind paste

²/₃ cup water

¼ cup plus 2 tablespoons brown sugar or jaggery

⅛ teaspoon chili powder

1½ teaspoons ground cumin

½ teaspoon salt

½ teaspoon freshly ground black pepper

STEPS

1. In a small saucepan, dissolve tamarind paste in water over medium heat. Add brown sugar and cayenne pepper and bring to a boil. Then simmer until it is less syrupy. Add cumin, salt and pepper. Adjust seasoning according to taste.

My mom usually served samosas with a green chutney (made with cilantro and mint) and a sour-sweet tamarind chutney that had a spicy bite. But if she ran out of time, we would have them with her homemade ketchup.

These days when I make samosas, I follow my mother's recipe for the potato-pea filling but with a few tweaks. I use less garam masala and add crushed fennel and ground cinnamon. If I am on a time crunch, I use puff pastry sheets instead of making dough from scratch. And yes, I too bring out the ketchup.

Sour Cream Chicken Cheese Enchiladas

Makes 24

Contributed by
Carolyn Fronapel

(from a recipe of
Jean Wyzykowski)

Here is another recipe from one of my dear friends from church, Carolyn Fronapel. Our congregation (and especially the choir) are more like an extended family. We spend a lot of time together at weddings and funerals, baptisms and birthdays. And almost all of them involve long tables groaning with casseroles and the specialties we have come to expect from each other. I have to bring pepperoni rolls and Carolyn has to bring the cheesy chicken enchiladas. And she is always anxious to credit Jean Wyzykowski for the original recipe.

INGREDIENTS

2 pounds boneless chicken breasts, boiled and diced

2 pints sour cream

4 cans cream of chicken soup

1 onion, chopped fine

1 pound longhorn or Cheddar cheese, shredded

2 packages flour tortillas (24)

STEPS

1. Preheat the oven to 375 degrees F.

2. Combine the chicken, sour cream, soup, onion and half of the cheese. Put about 2 tablespoons of filling on each tortilla, top with a little shredded cheese and roll up. Place seam side down in a 9 x 13-inch baking dish. Use the remainder of the mixture to cover the enchiladas and sprinkle with the remaining cheese. Bake for 30 to 45 minutes.

Timpano

8 to 10 servings

In the Stanley Tucci movie, "The Big Night," he and his brother's character create a mind-blowing tower of pasta called a "timpano" (or drum) in order to impress Louis Prima and gain notoriety for their small restaurant in New Jersey. Louis never shows up. But the timpano is magnificent. This is my take on the recipe, using both pastas and risotto in the layers to form the colors of the Italian flag. Yes, it is showy, but also delicious and an appropriate centerpiece for any festive occasion. I'm still waiting for Louis Prima to show up.

INGREDIENTS

DOUGH:

6 cups all-purpose flour

1 teaspoon salt

2 tablespoons baking powder

½ pound butter, softened

1½ cups granulated sugar

8 eggs

1 egg yolk mixed with 1 tablespoon water (for egg wash)

FILLINGS (5 LAYERS):

1 pound of penne cooked very al dente and tossed with pesto sauce

1 pound prepared risotto mixed with 1 bag frozen peas

8 hard boiled eggs

1 pound small meatballs, fried and cooked in tomato sauce

1 pound of ziti cooked very al dente and tossed with 2 cups of tomato sauce

1 quart tomato basil sauce for serving

STEPS

1. Preheat the oven to 350 degrees F.

2. Put flour, salt and baking powder in a mixing bowl and mix at lowest speed. Cut in butter and continue to mix until texture resembles fine cornmeal. Add sugar and mix. Add the 8 eggs one at a time and continue mixing at low speed just until a dough forms and pulls away from the side of the bowl. Be careful not to overwork the dough.

3. Remove dough and shape into a ball. Remove and set aside ¼ of the dough for the top crust. On a floured surface, roll the larger ball into a circle approximately 16 inches in diameter. Roll the circle up on your rolling pin and unroll into a 9-inch mixing bowl which has been liberally greased or sprayed with non-stick, covering the bottom and sides. Pinch off excess dough leaving a 1/4-inch overhang.

4. Add the fillings in even layers one at a time, starting with the penne al pesto, followed by the risotto, eggs, meatballs and ziti.

5. Roll the reserved dough into a 10-inch circle and place on top of the final layer. Crimp the edges to seal like a pie crust. Bake for 1 hour. Halfway through baking, cover bowl with foil to prevent burning or over-browning.

6. Remove from the oven and let rest for at least 20 minutes. Invert the bowl onto a large cutting board or serving platter. With a serrated knife cut the timpano into 1- or 2-inch wedges. Ladle some warm sauce on a plate and place the wedge of timpano on top. Top with additional sauce and grated cheese if desired.

Pizza Rustica

24 servings

Most of the dishes I enjoyed as a child came from my mother's Sicilian food traditions. But there were a few specialties that came from my father's side of the family. His sister, Mamie, used to make this Italian quiche for the holidays and my mother adopted the recipe. She used to ask the grocer on the corner to save the ends of the cold cuts, to save a few cents on the preparation costs. I just ask them to cut the meats in ¼-inch slices to make it easier to dice. With all the eggs and cheese, this is a very dense preparation so a little bit goes a long way. We usually serve it cold as an appetizer or snack but you can certainly heat up a slice in the toaster oven.

INGREDIENTS

DOUGH:

3 cups flour

1 teaspoon salt

1⅛ cup warm water (110 degrees F.)

1 package rapid rise yeast

1 teaspoon sugar

⅛ cup olive oil

FILLING:

3 pounds ricotta

12 eggs

1 pound ham

¼ pound capicola

¼ pound Genoa salami

¼ pound hot pepperoni

¼ pound sharp provolone

¼ pound Jarlsberg or Swiss

¼ pound mozzarella

STEPS

1. In the bowl of a food processor add the flour and salt. In a measuring cup add warm water, yeast, sugar and oil. When the mixture starts to foam, turn on processor and add liquid all at once. Process for 20 seconds. Turn dough out onto lightly floured surface. Shape into a ball, then place in a large oiled bowl. Cover with plastic wrap and allow to rise until doubled in size. Voila! Pizza dough.

2. Preheat the oven to 350 degrees F.

3. *For the filling:* Mix ricotta and eggs. Chop the cold meats, shred the cheeses and add both to the ricotta-egg mixture.

4. Cut off 1/3 of the dough and reserve. Roll the larger piece of dough into a rectangle 15 x 19 inches. Line a 9 x 13-inch deep-sided, greased casserole with the dough. Pour in ingredients. Roll the remaining dough into a 10 x 14-inch rectangle and place on top, sealing and crimping the edges.

5. Brush the top with a beaten egg for a shiny finish. Cut a few small holes in the top to allow steam to escape and bake until the dough is golden brown and the mixture has set, about 1½ hours. Let it set for at least 20 minutes to firm up. Eat hot or cold.

PART TWO

VEGGIES

Stuffed vegetables are an ingenious and effective way to combine and infuse flavors. Chopped meat is just that — chopped meat — until you mix it with rice and surround it with a blanket of soft, pungent cabbage and then bathe it in a sweet and sour tomato broth. It's also a method to bring delicious economy to the table. Perhaps that's why there are so many stuffed vegetable recipes in our immigrant experience.

When I grew up in the 1950s, my mother and grandmother were always looking for a way to feed us well but inexpensively. Eggplant served as an economical substitute for more expensive meats. It was roasted, fried, sliced and made into casseroles. And the same can be said for cultures all across the European continent, especially around the Mediterranean.

In our neighborhood, many of the homes had little gardens where they grew their own tomatoes, zucchini, peppers and eggplant. But to take full advantage of the bounty, the cooks relied on favorite recipes to transform them from their humble place on the vine to luscious entrees.

Stuffed Zucchini

4 servings

As the days dwindle down to a precious few in September, the zukes take on a ponderous look. The skins are tough and the centers are filled with seeds and water. The good news is that the price is right. For zucchini bread I peel them and cut them lengthwise into quarters, then scrape the seeds out and coarsely shred the flesh. These jumbo zucchini are also fine for soups and stews where the additional water content will not hurt the final dish.

But my favorite dish at this time of year is stuffed zucchini. There are hundreds of potential fillings for these jolly green giants of the vegetable world. The following recipe makes a vegetarian main course that goes well with a side of rice, couscous or pasta.

INGREDIENTS

2 cups plain breadcrumbs

4 tablespoons plus 1 tablespoon olive oil, divided

1 tablespoon capers

1 large zucchini (2–3 pounds)

1 medium onion, diced

1 clove garlic

1 large tomato, diced

1 green pepper, diced

1 teaspoon oregano

Salt and pepper to taste

1 teaspoon red pepper flakes (optional)

Juice of 1 lemon

½ cup grated pecorino Romano cheese

STEPS

1. Preheat the oven to 350 degrees F.

2. In a heavy skillet over medium heat, brown the breadcrumbs, stirring constantly until they are a light amber color. Moisten with the 4 tablespoons of olive oil and stir in the capers.

3. Cut the zucchinis in half lengthwise. Carefully scrape out the flesh, leaving a shell about 1/4-inch thick. Heat the additional tablespoon of oil in a large skillet and fry the zucchini you scraped from the shell. When it starts to brown, add the onion and then the garlic, tomato and pepper. Continue cooking until most of the moisture has evaporated. Add the oregano, salt and pepper and red pepper to taste. Turn off the heat and stir in the breadcrumb mixture, lemon juice and grated cheese.

4. Divide the mixture in half and fill each of the zucchini shells. Bake on a greased jelly roll pan for about 25 minutes until the shell is tender but not falling apart.

Stuffed Cabbage Rolls

Makes about 24

Family food traditions don't always originate in the country of that family's heritage. I knew a German/ Czechoslovakian family who celebrated each Thanksgiving with an enormous Chinese feast. Irish families in my Italian neighborhood came home to spaghetti every Wednesday night. America is the great melting pot of cultures and so is the American kitchen. Since the first settlers shared recipes with the Native Americans, fusion cuisine has been alive and well in this country.

One year, my father rented a little summer bungalow on Long Island. In the unit next door was a young Polish woman with her husband and little baby. Over the course of the summer, Mom shared many of her Italian favorites like pasta with squash and cream puffs with cream made from sweetened ricotta cheese. And to my father's delight, Mom learned authentic recipes for pierogi and stuffed cabbage rolls — "golubki."

INGREDIENTS

1 large head of cabbage

FILLING:

1 large onion, finely diced

1 red pepper, finely diced

2 tablespoons butter

½ pound ground beef

½ pound ground pork

1 cup uncooked rice

Salt and pepper

1 (28-ounce) can plum tomatoes, put through a food mill to have a sauce consistency

1 jar Heinz Chili Sauce

1 cup grape jelly

STEPS

1. Core the cabbage and put in boiling salted water to cover. As the outer leaves soften, remove them with tongs. Trim, but don't completely remove the thick stem on each leaf, so that they will roll more evenly. Set the leaves aside.

2. *For the filling:* Sauté the onions and pepper in butter over a medium-low heat until tender. Add the ground beef, pork and rice along with 1/4 cup of the tomato sauce to moisten. Salt and pepper to taste.

To assemble:

1. Preheat the oven to 350 degrees F.

2. Starting at the stem end of each leaf, put 1/4 cup of the mixture near the edge. Roll over the mixture, turn in the right and left sides and continue to roll until you form a bundle. Don't pack too tightly because the rice will expand. Place seam side down in a large covered roaster. Continue stuffing and rolling leaves.

3. Chop up any remaining cabbage and fill in between the rolls. Mix the rest of the tomato sauce with the chili sauce and grape jelly and heat until the jelly melts. Pour over the cabbage rolls. If necessary, add water until the rolls are just covered. Bake, covered, for 1½ hours. Remove the cover and cook for another 30 minutes to reduce the sauce.

Vegetarian option: You can substitute another protein for the 16 ounces of ground meat in this recipe. I would suggest 2 cans of well-drained red kidney beans.

Dad had grown up in a Polish/Italian area of Brooklyn between the parishes of Our Lady of Czestachowa and Saint Rocco's. He went to confession at the Polish church so the priest wouldn't understand his sins and communion at the Italian church where he could understand the sermon. But the foods he enjoyed equally.

Over the years I've tinkered with my mother's version of cabbage rolls and borrowed from others. At this point I'm not sure if the recipe is more Polish or Hungarian or Russian, but I have kept the little touch of Italian love she put in everything she made.

Stuffed Zucchini Blossoms

4 to 6 appetizer servings

Contributed by
**Dave and Aimee D'Anoia,
D'Anoia's Eatery, Pittsburgh**

*Dave: Squash blossoms have
always been in my family
and my wife's family — from
making and stuffing them when
we were kids, all the way to
traveling to Italy and stuffing
pancakes with the blossoms.
They are always the most
delicate and flavorful part of
the squash. From parents to
cousins and aunts and uncles,
it was always a little bit of a
competition for who had the
best stuffed squash blossoms.
And now this has become
my recipe.*

INGREDIENTS

**12 squash blossoms/
zucchini flowers**

2 quarts canola oil

FILLING:

1 quart ricotta cheese

4 eggs

**2 tablespoons garlic
powder**

**2 tablespoons onion
powder**

1 tablespoon oregano

1 tablespoon dried basil

BATTER:

3 cups seltzer water

4 cups AP flour

STEPS

1. Pull out and discard the pistil from the
   center of each flower and set the flowers
   aside.

2. Heat oil in a small saucepan until it
   reaches 350 degrees F.

3. Combine filling ingredients in a bowl and
   whisk until all is incorporated. Place in a
   piping bag and set aside.

4. Whisk together batter ingredients until
   all is incorporated

5. Take your squash blossoms and pull
   the petals apart so you can fit the tip of
   the bag in the top. Squeeze the ricotta
   mixture into the flower until it is filled
   and leave a little room so you can twist
   the top just a little. Dip in the batter and
   let the excess drip off.

6. Drop into the oil and fry until golden
   brown, about 2 to 3 minutes on either
   side. Remove and let sit on a paper towel
   to let the excess oil come off and the
   fried squash blossom cool down and
   crisp. Let rest for a minute then serve
   and enjoy.

Stuffed Tomatoes

8 servings

My great-grandfather, Giovanni Bacchi, and his oldest daughter, Marie (my grandmother), owned two houses that sat at a 90-degree angle to each other. In the space where they met at the back, Papa built a grape arbor to shelter our Summer Sunday dinners and a garden where he could grow tomatoes, zucchini, peppers, basil, parsley and figs. That garden provided a bounty every fall and this stuffed tomato recipe was always attributed to Papa.

INGREDIENTS

8 medium tomatoes

FILLING:

1 onion, finely chopped

½ cup olive oil

2–3 anchovies

2 tablespoons fresh parsley, chopped fine

1 tablespoon capers

1 cup breadcrumbs

Salt and pepper

STEPS

1. Preheat the oven to 400 degrees F.

2. Cut a small "X" in the bottom of each tomato and drop it into boiling water for 1 minute. Rinse in cold water and remove the skins. They should peel off easily. Carefully cut the tops from the tomatoes and reserve. Use a spoon to scoop out the seeds and sprinkle each with a little salt. Leave inverted on paper towel to drain.

3. *For the filling:* Fry the chopped onions in 1/4 cup of the oil until they are soft. Remove from the heat and stir in the anchovies, parsley, capers, 2 tablespoons of the breadcrumbs and a little black pepper. Fill the tomatoes with the mixture. Top with the tomato lids and place in an oiled baking pan.

4. Heat the remaining oil and toast the rest of the breadcrumbs until brown. Sprinkle over the tomatoes in the pan. Cover with foil and bake for 30 minutes.

Vegetarian option: If you choose not to use the anchovy in this recipe you might want to kick up the flavor with a little extra herbs and spices such as oregano, red pepper flakes or even curry!

Loaded Potatoes

8 servings

In the land of Comfort Food, the potato is king! Baked, boiled, mashed, fried and roasted, they have consistently remained one of the most versatile and economical staples in the pantry. Many Sundays, my mom would make a mashed potato casserole to accompany the chicken or roast beef we had after the pasta course. This recipe takes advantage of all the delicious flavors of that recipe and puts it into neat individual servings.

INGREDIENTS

6 large Idaho baking potatoes

4 tablespoons butter

¼ cup milk

4 slices Genoa salami, diced

½ cup grated pecorino Romano cheese

½ pound low moisture mozzarella, diced

2 tablespoons chopped fresh parsley

Salt and pepper

STEPS

1. Preheat the oven to 400 degrees F.

2. Rinse and dry the potatoes and prick with the tines of a fork in several places to keep them from exploding. Roast the potatoes for at least an hour until a knife goes in smoothly. Cut each potato in half lengthwise and scoop out into a bowl while still warm and leaving about 1/8-inch of potato on the skin. Add the butter and stir until melted. Add the milk and salami and mix well.

3. Let cool to room temperature, then stir in the small cubes of mozzarella, the pecorino Romano and parsley. Put a generous amount of filling into 8 of the potato skins. Put a small pat of butter on top of each. Place on a baking sheet and bake for 20 to 30 minutes until the tops begin to brown and the centers are hot (200 degrees F).

Note: I don't like to waste the other 4 potato skins so I usually brush them with olive oil, give them a dusting of coarse salt and crisp them in the oven while the other potatoes are cooking.

Vegetarian option: Of course you can leave out the salami but it would be nice to add some diced red pepper for flavor and color.

Bacon-Wrapped Stuffed Jalapeños

Makes 12

Contributed by

Julie Mueller

When we did a cooking special dedicated to recipes that use bacon, my son, Joseph, and his fiance, Julie, came on the show to demonstrate a spicy appetizer they like to make for their friends. Joe remarked that you will never know how these tasty mouthfuls would be reheated the next day — there are never any leftovers!

INGREDIENTS

12 jalapeños, about 3-4 inches long

4 ounces cream cheese

12 slices bacon (one for each pepper)

STEPS

1. Preheat the oven to broil on high.

2. Slice the tops off of the peppers and halve them lengthwise, cleaning out seeds as you go. Fill the pepper halves with cream cheese, leveling off the cream cheese with your finger so that the pepper isn't overstuffed.

3. Cut the slices of bacon in half and wrap each piece around the pepper and secure with a toothpick. Broil on high for about 15 minutes or until bacon begins to char.

TIPS

- If you're working with a block of cream cheese, try cutting it into slices to make it easier to work with; this also makes for less of a mess!

- When wrapping the peppers with bacon, try to make sure you seal off the open end with the piece of bacon so that the cream cheese can't run out.

- Try to avoid touching your eyes after handling the jalapeños; it might be useful to wear a pair of food-safe gloves.

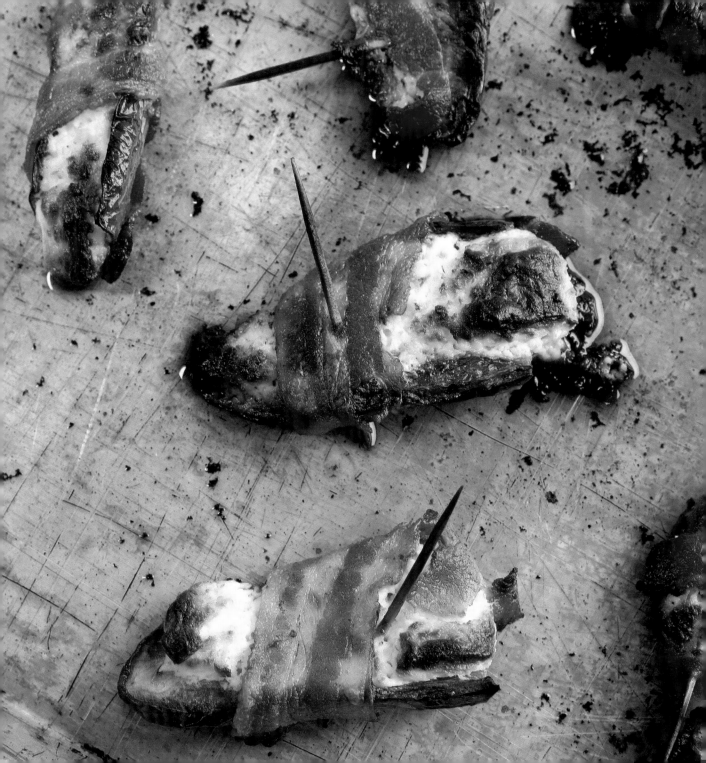

Stuffed Artichokes

4 servings

This dish was a specialty of my grandmother, Marie Felice. Her father came from Monreale, a little town near Palermo, Sicily. Gram was the oldest of eight sisters and she had to leave school around the age of twelve to take care of her siblings. But she knew how to read and write and she taught herself all she needed to know. She was a genius of a seamstress and a magician in the kitchen. She followed no recipes except those in her head and this artichoke dish was one of her specialties. It was served as a sort of first course after antipasti and before pasta. It's deliciously messy to eat. You pull off one leaf at a time and scrape the moist filling into your mouth along with the little bit of soft artichoke at the bottom of the leaf. When you finally get to the center you have to scrape out the choke and you can then eat the tender heart. Heaven.

INGREDIENTS

4 large artichokes

2 lemons

FILLING:

2 cups dry breadcrumbs

4 tablespoons olive oil

6 anchovies

1 tablespoon capers

STEPS

1. Preheat the oven to 350 degrees F.

2. Cut the stem off each artichoke to provide a flat bottom and remove some of the tough outer leaves. Use a scissors to trim the prickly points from the top of the leaves. Use a sharp knife to cut 1 inch from the top of each artichoke. Put the trimmed artichokes in a large bowl of water to cover, into which you have added the juice of 1 lemon and the lemon rinds.

3. *For the filling:* In a large, heavy skillet over medium heat, toast the breadcrumbs until they are amber colored. Reduce the heat and add the olive oil, anchovies and capers, stirring to break up the anchovies. Allow to cool.

4. Begin stuffing the artichokes starting from the outside leaves and working towards the center. Place in a high-sided casserole dish that will just fit the artichokes standing up. Pour enough water into the bottom of the pan to come up about 1 inch.

5. Squeeze the juice of the second lemon on top of the artichokes and bake for at least an hour, until the tops are lightly browned and the bottoms are tender enough to be pierced easily with a toothpick.

Note: Do not put your fingers in your mouth after handling the raw artichokes. They have a most bitter taste.

Vegetarian option: You can omit the anchovies but you'll need to increase the salt and spices.

Stuffed Mushrooms

Makes 24

This was another favorite of my grandmother. She even had special metal trays that she used to bake them until the mushrooms were infused with the bacon and cheese flavoring of the stuffing.

INGREDIENTS

24 large mushrooms (2 inches across)

FILLING:

2 slices bacon

1 small onion

½ cup breadcrumbs

1 teaspoon parsley

¼ cup pecorino Romano cheese, grated

Salt and pepper to taste

Juice of 1 lemon

¼ cup olive oil

¼ cup water

STEPS

1. Preheat the oven to 350 degrees F.

2. Trim the end of the stems and remove them from the mushroom caps. Clean or peel the mushroom caps and set aside.

3. *For the filling:* Chop the bacon into small dice and fry until the fat is rendered. Chop the mushroom stems and the onion and add them to the skillet. Sauté until the onion is brown. Remove from the heat and stir in the breadcrumbs, parsley and cheese. Season with salt and pepper to taste. Moisten the mixture with the lemon juice and half the olive oil.

4. Fill the mushroom caps and place them in a baking dish with the water on the bottom. Drizzle with the remaining oil and bake for 30 to 40 minutes until the mushrooms are cooked and the filling is browned.

Vegetarian option: To get the bacon flavor without the meat, try McCormick's® Bac'n Pieces or other bacon-flavored bits.

Stuffed Banana Peppers

Makes 12

When I moved to Pittsburgh from New York in 1985 I was introduced to a whole new world of culinary favorites. Back in Brooklyn no one had ever heard of Turkey Devonshire, Chipped Ham or putting french fries and coleslaw on top of your sandwich. It seemed like every restaurant included versions of fried zucchini and stuffed banana peppers on their appetizer menus. This version comes from one of Pittsburgh's finest chefs, Pat Joyce, when his restaurant on the South Side of town was called the 17th Street Grill.

INGREDIENTS

1 dozen yellow hot peppers

FILLING:

2 pounds ground meat (you can use veal, chicken, turkey or pork)

1 tablespoon dry basil

½ tablespoon dry oregano

½ tablespoon dry thyme

3 eggs

1 tablespoon minced garlic

Salt and pepper

2 cups panko breadcrumbs

1 cup water

2 cups marinara sauce

1 cup shredded provolone

1 cup shredded mozzarella

STEPS

1. Preheat the oven to 350 degrees F. Put on rubber gloves.

2. Using a knife, make a slice about 1/2 inch from top of each pepper but don't cut all the way through. Cut from that line to the tip and remove the seeds. Place peppers to the side.

3. *For the filling:* In a mixing bowl, place the ground meat, spices, eggs, garlic, salt and pepper and breadcrumbs, and mix by hand. It should be the consistency of a meatball.

4. Fill the peppers with the meat stuffing. Place the stuffed peppers in a 9 x 10-inch baking pan with 1 cup of water and cover with foil. Bake for approximately 45 minutes or to an internal temperature of 170 degrees F.

5. Remove from oven and carefully drain the water. Pour your favorite marinara sauce and top with shredded cheese. Place back in oven to melt the cheese. Remove from oven and serve this Pittsburgh Classic.

Stuffed Sweet Cubanella Peppers

Makes 12 to 18

Here's a recipe from my friend Joseph Certo. He shared it with the WQED viewers when we did a program called "H" Is for Harvest. These stuffed cubanella peppers were so delicious on the program that I went home and made them the next day. I've been making them regularly ever since.

INGREDIENTS

12–18 cubanella peppers

FILLING:

2 cups seasoned breadcrumbs

½ cup chopped black olives

½ cup chopped green stuffed olives

2–3 plum tomatoes, seeded and chopped

1 cup Asiago cheese

½ cup grated pecorino Romano cheese

2 eggs

¼ cup olive oil, plus oil for frying

STEPS

1. Preheat the oven to 350 degrees F.

2. Cut tops off peppers and clean out seeds.

3. *For the filling:* Mix all the remaining ingredients except eggs and olive oil in a large bowl. Beat the eggs with the olive oil in a small bowl. Pour egg and oil mixture over dry ingredients and stir.

4. Stuff mixture into peppers. Fry peppers slowly in the additional olive oil over low heat, turning frequently to brown all sides. Bake until they are tender, about an hour.

Note: Frying does impart a special flavor to these peppers, but if you are trying to reduce fat in your diet you can simply brush the stuffed peppers with a little olive oil and then bake.

Stuffed Eggplant Rolls

4 to 6 servings

I often joke that when I was growing up, we thought of eggplant as "the other dark meat." Part of that was the frugality of my mother and grandmother and the other was their Sicilian kitchen traditions. Gram made huge bowls of caponatina (a kind of Sicilian version of ratatouille) and kept it in the fridge ready for sandwiches or side dishes.

Most of our vegetables came to us by way of Ralph. He came around the neighborhood with a cart pulled by his horse, Babe. I can remember Gram standing there with two perfect, shiny eggplants, turning them this way and that to assess which was the more perfect! Poor Ralph.

INGREDIENTS

3 globe eggplants, cut crosswise into ¼-inch-thick rounds

½ cup extra virgin olive oil, or as needed

Salt

Freshly ground black pepper

FILLING:

½ cup fine dried breadcrumbs

½ cup grated pecorino or provolone cheese

¼ cup chopped fresh flat leaf parsley or equal parts parsley and basil

2 or 3 cloves garlic, finely minced

1 tablespoon grated lemon zest (optional)

Salt

Freshly ground black pepper

STEPS

1. To fry the eggplant slices, place them in a colander, lightly salting the layers, and let stand for 30 minutes to drain. Pat the eggplant slices completely dry with paper towels. In a sauté pan, heat the olive oil over medium heat. Working in batches, add the eggplant slices and fry, turning once, until translucent and tender but not too soft, 6 to 8 minutes total. Transfer to paper towels to drain. Repeat with the remaining slices.

2. Preheat the oven to 400 degrees F.

3. *For the filling:* In a bowl, combine the breadcrumbs, cheese, parsley, garlic, and the lemon zest, if using, and mix well. Season to taste with salt and pepper.

4. Divide the breadcrumb mixture evenly among the eggplant slices, spreading it evenly on each. Roll up the slices and secure with toothpicks if they won't stay rolled.

5. Lightly oil a baking dish (or a flameproof dish if using the broiler) large enough to accommodate the eggplant rolls in a single layer. Arrange the rolls, seam side down, in the dish. Drizzle the rolls with olive oil. Place the dish in the oven and bake for 15 to 20 minutes. Remove the toothpicks, if used, and arrange the rolls on a platter. Serve warm or at room temperature.

Stuffed Pumpkin

6 to 8 servings

Contributed by
Mary Ann Williams

Mary Ann: I got this recipe around 1979 when I was a Tupperware Manager in a distributorship that was in Warrendale (Pa.) back then. Over the years I made this for my family almost every year in October. My kids have always loved it...even though 'everything is mixed together'! I was born in October as well as my first-born child. This Dinner-In-A-Pumpkin is almost a part of our family tradition, and one of the traditional things I make in November for Thanksgiving. When the kids went to college, I always tried to time the making of this meal for a weekend when at least a few of them would be home.

This recipe is for a pumpkin slightly bigger than a basketball. If the pumpkin is larger or smaller, of course, the volume of the filling would need to be adjusted accordingly.

INGREDIENTS

FILLING:

3 pounds ground beef

1 large onion

2 green peppers

About 2 cups chopped celery

Salt and pepper to taste

¼ cup soy sauce

2 tablespoons brown sugar

1 (4-ounce) can sliced mushrooms OR use fresh mushrooms

¾ cup cream

¾–1 cup chicken broth or stock

2 cups uncooked rice

1 pumpkin

STEPS

1. Preheat the oven to 375 degrees F.

2. *For the filling:* In a large pan on the stove, brown the ground beef. While it's browning, add the peppers, celery salt and pepper. Drain the meat. Stir in the soy sauce, sugar, mushrooms, cream, broth and rice.

3. Cut the top off of the pumpkin just as you would for the start of a jack-o-lantern project. Save the "lid." Clean the seeds and pulp from the inside. (Resist the temptation to cut out a face!) Rinse out the inside of the pumpkin a bit.

4. Spoon the meat mixture into the pumpkin. Place the top back on the pumpkin. Set the pumpkin on a sheet pan with low sides. Roast for about an hour or until the pumpkin is tender. Can take less or more than an hour depending on the thickness of the walls of the pumpkin.

5. As you serve dinner, be sure to scoop the inside of the pumpkin along with the meat mixture. Yum! This is delicious with a side of homemade applesauce and fresh bread.

Stuffed Acorn Squash

4 servings

Contributed by
Joseph Fennimore

Joseph: This is an instant fall classic, and my favorite thing to do with winter squash. Each half ends up being a perfect personal portion, and the stuffing is incredibly flavorful and satisfying. If your acorn squash are small, don't worry; this works just fine if you don't split it in half and instead cut into the seed cavity from the top like you'd get to the center of a pumpkin.

For cutting the squash in half horizontally, it can be tricky, but I usually find that by rocking the knife a bit in its groove (rather than sawing) I eventually make progress. Also, for extra flavor, I sometimes use hot sausage. The spice adds a nice kick and is generally balanced by the sweetness from the apple, cheese, and the squash itself.

INGREDIENTS

2 medium acorn squash

FILLING:

1 onion

1 tablespoon olive oil

1 teaspoon salt

1 teaspoon pepper

1 teaspoon rosemary

½ pound loose sausage

3 cloves garlic, minced

1 apple, peeled and diced

½ cup walnuts

1 cup breadcrumbs

½ cup pecorino Romano or Parmigiano cheese

STEPS

1. Preheat the oven to 400 degrees F.

2. Cut off the top and very bottom of the squash to flatten the top and the bottom. Then cut the squash in half horizontally to create halves that sit on the flat surfaces of the top and bottom. Scrape out seeds, drizzle with olive oil, top with salt and pepper, and bake for 45 to 50 minutes.

3. *For the filling:* Dice onion and sauté in olive oil until translucent. Add rosemary and cook until fragrant. Add sausage and garlic and cook over medium high heat until sausage is cooked.

4. Add apple cubes and the walnuts, crushed to smaller pieces.

5. Remove from heat and add breadcrumbs and cheese. Cheese should melt and breadcrumbs will pick up all juices in the pan. When the squash is done, spoon the filling into each pocket, then top with more grated cheese. Put the stuffed squash back in the oven for 20 minutes.

Vegetarian option: There are several brands of vegetarian sausage that will provide the right flavors for this dish.

Meat-Stuffed Grape Leaves (Dolmathes)

Makes about 100 rolls

In the backyard of my house there is a very small grape arbor that produces the most bitter and inedible grapes I have ever tried. But it is a beautiful and prodigious producer of grape leaves. My dear friend Kweilin Nassar showed me how to harvest the leaves, blanch and then freeze them for use throughout the year. The recipe calls for commercially purchased grape leaves but if you have a friend with a grape arbor...

When I first got this recipe I thought that 100 was an excessive amount. Then I realized that every person can eat between 10 and 20 of these delicious mouthfuls. It is best to make these as a group project to cut down on the prep time.

INGREDIENTS

2 (16-ounce) jars grape leaves (about 100)

FILLING:

2 cups finely chopped onions

1½ cups finely chopped celery

1 cup olive oil

2½ pounds ground meat

4 cups rice

½ cup chopped fresh parsley

½ cup chopped fresh dill or mint (or 1 tablespoon dried)

2 teaspoons salt

1 teaspoon pepper

5 quarts chicken broth

1 cup lemon juice

STEPS

1. Rinse and drain grape leaves thoroughly. Trim stems if necessary.

2. *For the filling:* Sauté the onions and celery in 1/2 cup of the olive oil until soft. In a large bowl, combine the onion/celery mixture with the remaining 7 stuffing ingredients and stir until well mixed.

3. Place 1 heaping teaspoon of meat mixture just below the center of a leaf. Fold the bottom of the leaf over the filling; fold the sides in over the filling, then roll the leaf into a small oblong package. Do not fold too tightly, since the rice will swell when it cooks.

4. Lay the stuffed leaves in the bottom of a heavy, large-sized saucepan, fitting them together neatly, but not too tightly. Combine chicken broth and lemon juice. Pour the broth mixture over the grape leaves, covering them just to the top. Place a heavy plate, slightly smaller than the diameter of the saucepan, over the leaves to keep them from shifting during cooking.

5. Cook over low heat, simmering about 45 minutes, until meat is cooked and rice is tender. Garnish with a drizzle of olive oil and lemon wedges.

Vegetarian option: Many people fill these grape leaves with just the rice and not the meat. The flavors and textures are still very good.

Italian Stuffed Green Olives

Makes 30

Contributed by
Karen Tracy

This recipe and its heart-warming story came to us for our program about Italian recipes.

Karen: I have always been so proud of my Italian heritage but never so much as this past year when my 92-year-old grandmother passed away just 15 days before Christmas. Being Italian and devoted Catholics, Christmas Eve was religiously a solemn day of fasting followed by Christmas Day — a joyous celebration of family, love and tradition. We sensed that Grandma Katie would want us to celebrate her favorite holiday as she had for 73 years — with Pappy's stuffed olives topping the Christmas Day menu. At age 17, Pappy immigrated from a tiny village on the Adriatic Sea — Ascoli Piceno, Italy — and introduced his mother's cherished recipe to Carnegie, Pennsylvania. I'm reminded of him seated at our kitchen table, sipping a small glass of homemade wine, meticulously

INGREDIENTS

30 giant green olives

FILLING:

1 pound ground chuck

1 cup grated Parmigiano cheese

2 eggs

¼ cup water

1 teaspoon grated lemon zest

1 clove finely chopped garlic

Chopped parsley

½ teaspoon salt

¼ teaspoon black pepper

½ cup cracker meal

COATING:

1 cup flour

2 beaten eggs

2 cups cracker meal

Oil for frying

STEPS

1. With a sharp paring knife, remove the olive pits in a circular movement (like peeling an apple into a spiral) from the top to bottom.

2. *For the filling:* Mix meat, cheese, eggs, water, lemon zest, garlic, parsley, salt and pepper and 1/2 cup cracker meal. Roll into small balls and insert in the olive spiral. Refrigerate for at least an hour.

3. Roll each stuffed olive in flour to coat. Dip into beaten eggs, then cracker meal. Deep fry in hot oil until golden brown. Sprinkle with grated cheese and enjoy!

removing with the sharp paring knife the olive pit, in the same manner as peeling an apple — in a circular movement without breaking the spiral, from the top to the bottom of a mammoth green olive. My sister and I, supervised by Grandma Katie, would roll tiny meatballs to be later stuffed into his "green ribbons," then fried to a delicious golden brown.

Pappy's gentle hands, carefully peeling the olives and Grandma's hands clapping while she joyfully danced around her kitchen singing Italian Christmas carols, will forever be a loving remembrance of our childhood. My sister and I will celebrate next Christmas with our own husbands and children, but without Grandma and Pappy. Their green olives always highlighted our Christmas dinners and will continue to be a meaningful ingredient of our family celebrations — "stuffed" with love and tradition.

Stuffed Bell Peppers

8 servings

Here's another one of my mother's recipes that she used to feed seven people on a weekly budget of just $20. The aroma of these peppers in the oven brings me right back to her little kitchen in Brooklyn!

INGREDIENTS

4 peppers

FILLING:

½ pound chopped meat

1 onion, chopped

1 cup cooked rice

½ cup grated pecorino Romano cheese

Parsley

Salt and pepper

1 egg

¼ cup breadcrumbs

Olive oil

STEPS

1. Preheat the oven to 350 degrees F.

2. Cut the peppers in half lengthwise and remove the stems, ribs and seeds. Place them in a baking dish.

3. *For the filling:* Brown the chopped meat then add the onions and sauté until soft. Add the rice, cheese and parsley and season with salt and pepper. Stir in the beaten egg.

4. Stuff the peppers and sprinkle with the breadcrumbs. Drizzle with olive oil and bake until the peppers are tender.

Vegetarian option: Instead of ground meat, use a mixture of cauliflower and walnuts that you have pulsed in a food processor.

PART THREE

BREAD & PASTRY

*T*he story goes that pepperoni rolls were devised to provide a nutritious snack for West Virginia coal workers that could be held in one hand as they were riding the tram cars down to the mines. My guess is that these early "hot-pockets" were being made long before the first coal mine in West Virginia. It just makes sense to jam some meat or cheese or vegetables into a blob of dough and then bake it until the center is all oozy and delicious. The French brought the technique to a fine art, encrusting everything from veggies to roast beef in a flaky pastry crust. But the same idea has been going on all over the world for centuries.

In times of crisis, people turn in different directions for consolation. I head straight for the kitchen. After 9/11, in a single twenty-four hour period I made: a chicken pot pie; crock pot beef stew with carrots and potatoes; Boston baked beans; a beef, pork and veal meatloaf with mashed potatoes; four dozen meatballs; tortellini; matzo ball soup; macaroni and cheese; a giant braided loaf of egg bread; and eight dozen cookies. I was finally slowed down by the limitations of my refrigerator.

When I was around ten years old, there was a terrible thunderstorm with high winds that knocked out the electricity and battered our house with sheets of driving rain. I distinctly remember falling into the grip of a senseless fear. Mom lit candles and started making pizza dough. My sisters and I gathered around the kitchen table as the yeasty aroma of the rising bread filled the room and sang songs so we couldn't hear the raging storm. By the time the pizza was ready, the storm had subsided and the lights returned. We were having so much fun that we turned the lights off and ate by the candlelight.

It's no wonder I associate food with comfort and consolation. And bread is at the top of my list for those comforting foods.

Sausage Rolls

Makes 24

The Fennimore clan has always been crazy for the sausage rolls my mother made for special occasions and holidays. She would usually bake up about 100 of the spicy little buns and that was never enough to satisfy the appetites of our family and friends. Her secret, as she passed on to us, was to fry the ground pork until it was brown and crunchy before draining and mixing with spices and cheeses and stuffing into the balls of dough. I learned to make my own version but I never mastered the art of getting in the maximum amount of filling or baking them as lightly as Mom did. We used to tease her and say she could make a million dollars if she would open up a shop and sell them. She said that if people had to pay for her time, the rolls would be too expensive.

INGREDIENTS

DOUGH:

1 tablespoon yeast

1 tablespoon sugar

1¼ cups warm water

¼ cup olive oil

3 cups flour

1 tablespoon salt

FILLING:

1½ pounds ground pork

1 teaspoon fennel seeds

Ground black pepper or red pepper flakes to taste

½ cup shredded sharp provolone

½ cup shredded mozzarella

¼ cup grated pecorino Romano cheese

STEPS

1. Preheat the oven to 350 degrees F.

2. *For the dough:* Dissolve the yeast and sugar in the warm water. Add the oil and let rest until the yeast gets foamy. Combine the flour and salt in the bowl of a mixer and add the yeast mixture. Mix until a dough forms, adding flour a tablespoon at a time until the dough is no longer sticky. Let rest for an hour.

   If making in a food processor, use the dough blade and combine the flour and salt in the processor. Turn on the machine and pour the liquids slowly through the feed tube just until a dough forms and begins to go around the outside of the bowl. Process for another 20 seconds and then let rest for an hour.

3. *For the filling:* Sauté the ground pork with the fennel seed and pepper in a large skillet until the meat is well browned. Drain and cool slightly. Mix in the cheeses.

4. Cut the dough into 24 pieces. Roll out each piece into a 3-inch circle. Place a tablespoon or more of the filling in the center of the circle and roll up, tucking in the sides. Place on parchment paper or in a greased baking pan. Allow to rise again for about 30 minutes. Bake until light brown.

Pepperoni Rolls

Makes 36

It feels like every child we know is graduating this year. Some will move from the relatively sheltered world of the elementary grades to the independent, soul-searching years of high school. Others will make the even more momentous leap to college with the prospect of moving out of the house. It is a proud moment for students and parents, but like any transition, it can be filled with anxiety. Will I fit in at the new school? Have I made the right choice? Will my little brother move into my room when I leave? Is the food in the cafeteria fit for human consumption?

Cafeteria food was never an issue for me. During the four years of my high school career I alternated between bologna and American cheese sandwiches, using both on special occasions. Pushing my tray past the steam table at college there always seemed to be three or four vats of similarly gray, creamy, lumpy things called "chicken ala king" or "beef stroganoff" or "turkey surprise" that was served over potatoes or rice or toast. It was

INGREDIENTS

½ stick butter

⅓ cup sugar

1½ cups milk, scalded

1 tablespoon yeast

⅓ cup lukewarm water (110 degrees F)

1 teaspoon sugar

1 egg, beaten

1 tablespoon salt

5 cups flour, divided

1 large pepperoni stick

1 egg, beaten for egg wash

STEPS

1. Add the butter and 1/3 cup sugar to the hot milk. Stir and allow to cool. Mix the yeast with the lukewarm water and the teaspoon of sugar. It should puff up in about five minutes. If you're using a stand mixer, you can put the flour and salt in the bowl and mix to combine. Then add the milk, egg and yeast mixture and use the dough hook for 6 to 8 minutes until the dough is smooth and comes away from the side of the bowl. Add 1 tablespoon of flour at a time if the dough is still too sticky. If working by hand, mix 4 cups of the flour with the other ingredients until a soft dough forms. Gradually add the rest of the flour and knead 8 to 10 minutes until smooth and elastic. Cover and let rise for 1 to 2 hours. Then cut the dough into 36 pieces.

2. Preheat the oven to 350 degrees F.

3. Peel the casing from the pepperoni and cut it into logs about 1/2 inch by 2 inches. Place a log on a piece of dough. Fold the sides in to the center and then roll up to form a bun that completely encloses the pepperoni. Place the rolls on greased cookie sheets and allow them to rise for an hour. Brush them with a beaten egg and bake for 15 to 20 minutes or until dark golden brown. Underbake them slightly if you are going to reheat them in the oven before serving.

my theory that they made an enormous batch of the same thing every night and just changed the signs. In any case, I survived both experiences and gained a new admiration for home cooking.

During my daughter, Maryann's, freshman year at the Rhode Island School of Design, we signed her up for the meal plan. I had visions of the same vats of glop from my college days. What we found was a wonderfully bright and open food court system where students could go to different "stations" for hot foods, vegetarian offerings, custom-made pastas or deli sandwiches, and enormous displays of fruits and breads. This was a food destination instead of a food disaster. It's nice to think that things have changed for the better.

I'd never even heard of these spicy little buns until I moved to Pittsburgh, and my wife swears the authentic versions come from West Virginia. I'll let you try these out and you can be the judge.

Calzone

About 8 sandwich-size servings

In my Brooklyn neighborhood of the 1950s and 1960s, it seemed like there was a pizza shop on every other corner. They served up the traditional New York slice (thin, and huge!) and two other dishes that used the same dough. One was the fried dough balls showered in powdered sugar called zeppole and the other was calzone. The filling usually included the meatier ham capicola plus ricotta and mozzarella but many offered meatless versions.

INGREDIENTS

DOUGH:

2 cups warm water (110-115 degrees F)

1 tablespoon active dry yeast

1 tablespoon sugar

¼ cup olive oil

1 tablespoon salt

4 cups all-purpose flour

FILLING:

1 pound ricotta cheese

½ cup pecorino Romano cheese, grated

½ cup mozzarella cheese, shredded

2 tablespoons fresh parsley, minced

1 egg, lightly beaten

½ teaspoon salt

¼ teaspoon black pepper

½ pound ham capicola, sliced thin

STEPS

1. Dissolve the yeast in the warm water with the sugar and olive oil. Allow to sit for 5 minutes until it foams. Put 3 cups of the flour into a large bowl and add the liquid. Stir vigorously with a wooden spoon for about 2 minutes. Add the salt to the batter and then gradually add enough flour to form a soft dough. Turn it out onto a floured surface and knead in enough flour to make a soft, smooth dough that barely sticks to your hands (about 8 minutes). Put in a lightly greased bowl, cover and allow to rise until double in size.

2. Preheat the oven to 400 degrees F.

3. Mix all the filling ingredients together except the ham.

4. Divide the dough into eight balls. Roll out each ball into an 8-inch circle. Cover half of each circle with slices of ham and 1/8 of the filling. Fold it over into a half-moon shape and crimp the edges tightly. Place them on a greased jelly roll pan and let them rest for 15 minutes. Poke a steam vent in the top of each calzone and bake for approximately 20 minutes or until deep golden brown.

You can alter the filling for this calzone recipe to suit your personal tastes. Try adding mushrooms or roasted red peppers or pepperoni or marinated artichoke hearts, etc. This is the way we made it in Brooklyn.

Pork Wellington

6 servings

Traditional Beef Wellington is an artful creation that rolls a tenderloin cut in patè studded with truffles and then a duxelle of mushrooms and finally bakes it encased in puff pastry — a sort of eighteenth century turducken. In the intervening years, the term has been more generally applied to any meat prepared "en croûte." This recipe is for a Pork Wellington that combines the traditional flavors of pork and sauerkraut. Most of the work can, and should, be done a day or two in advance. Then you just wrap the roast in pastry and bake it for an hour before dinner time. (For a Mini Beef Wellington recipe, see page 92.)

INGREDIENTS

2 pork tenderloins

Salt and pepper to taste

2 tablespoons olive oil

1 pound mushrooms, sliced

1 pound sauerkraut, rinsed and drained

1 teaspoon caraway seeds

12 slices cooked bacon

1 tablespoon coarse grain mustard

2 sheets puff pastry

1 egg beaten with 1 tablespoon water

STEPS

1. Trim all the fat and silver skin from the pork tenderloins. Pat dry on a paper towel and season with salt and pepper. Heat 1 tablespoon of the oil in a large skillet and brown the pork well on all sides, about 12 minutes. Remove from the skillet and let cool down.

2. Heat the remaining olive oil in the pan and sauté the mushrooms until they give up their moisture and begin to brown. Turn off the heat and add the rinsed and drained sauerkraut along with the caraway seeds. Stir to combine well and cool.

3. Lay out a sheet of clear plastic wrap on the counter. Place 6 strips of bacon on the wrap. Top with one-half of the sauerkraut and mushroom mixture and spread to cover the bacon, forming an 8 x 12-inch rectangle. Spread the mustard on the pork and place it along one long edge of the rectangle. Use the plastic wrap to help roll up the roast. Wrap tightly in the plastic wrap and refrigerate for at least 3 hours and up to 2 days. Repeat with the other tenderloin and mixture.

4. Preheat the oven to 375 degrees F.

5. Let the frozen puff pastry sheets sit at room temperature for about 40 minutes. Cut one sheet in half and roll out to approximately 14 x 10 inches. Brush a 2-inch border with some of the egg wash. Remove the plastic wrap from the tenderloin and place in the center of the puff pastry. Bring up the long sides to cover and press the seam. Place on a parchment-lined baking sheet. Tuck in the ends and press to seal. Decorate with cutouts of pastry or simply make designs with a sharp knife. Then brush with more of the egg wash. Repeat with the second tenderloin.

6. Bake for 30 minutes until the pastry is a deep golden brown and the thermometer registers at least 160 degrees F. Remove from the oven and let rest about 10 minutes before slicing into 1-inch rounds.

Mini Beef Wellington

4 servings

If you want to impress your dinner guests, this is the dish for you. It has a look of elegance, rich flavors of beef and mushroom and a recipe that can be staged so that you have time to enjoy the meal along with everyone else. The trickiest part for me is the cooking of the mushroom duxelle so that you remove the excess moisture before using it to surround the beef. But that can all be done the day before assembly.

INGREDIENTS

4 (4-ounce) beef tenderloin rounds, approx. 1-inch thick

Kosher salt to taste

Black pepper to taste

1 tablespoon canola oil

1 tablespoon whole grain mustard

THE DUXELLE:

8 ounces cremini mushrooms, sliced

Small onion, chopped

1 tablespoon butter

2 cloves garlic, minced

2 sheets puff pastry

8 slices prosciutto, thinly sliced, or ham

1 egg, beaten

STEPS

1. Let the beef come to room temperature. Season with kosher salt and pepper on all sides.

2. Add canola oil to a large pan on high heat. Once the oil is hot, add the rounds of steak. Cook about 3 minutes on each side without touching the steaks, to form a nice dark crust on each side. While it's still warm, brush the mustard on both sides of the meat. Let the meat rest while making the duxelle (mushrooms cooked and reduced until dry).

3. *For the duxelle:* Put the mushrooms and onion in a food processor and pulse until a smooth paste is formed. Melt the butter in the same pan you used to sear the meat and add the mushroom paste. Spread it evenly over the bottom of the pan and cook over medium heat until the mixture is nearly dry. Add the minced garlic and let the mixture cool completely.

4. Place a large layer of plastic wrap on your work surface. Cut each sheet of puff pastry into two pieces and roll each piece into a square. Lay two strips of prosciutto on each square. Spread a layer of the mushrooms evenly over the prosciutto. Place a piece of the tenderloin in the center of each square.

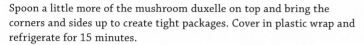

Spoon a little more of the mushroom duxelle on top and bring the corners and sides up to create tight packages. Cover in plastic wrap and refrigerate for 15 minutes.

5. Preheat the oven to 400 degrees F.

6. Place the packages on a greased, parchment paper-lined baking sheet. Brush the surface with the beaten eggs. With a fork, score a decorative design onto the surface of the puff pastry. Sprinkle with kosher salt. Bake for 40 minutes or until the puff pastry is a dark golden brown and the internal temperature of the beef is 135 degrees F for medium-rare.

Spanikopita

Makes 40 3-inch triangles

This version of spanikopita is a great way to get over what I call "Fear of Phyllo." The dough comes frozen in packages of folded sheets. Each sheet is so thin and fragile that it is easy to end up with a table full of phyllo shards instead of sheets. The trick is to work quickly and to keep the unused sheets covered with plastic wrap. Once the sheets are coated with melted butter they hold up fine and you can fold them without anxiety. The result is like a miracle: pastry that crackles and melts in your mouth at the same time.

INGREDIENTS

2 pounds frozen spinach

2 bunches scallions

4 eggs

1 pound feta cheese

1 tablespoon dried mint

Black pepper

1 pound phyllo dough

½ pound butter, melted

STEPS

1. Defrost the spinach and put into a sieve to drain. Press out as much moisture as possible. Chop the scallions, including the white tips and some of the light green stalks. Beat the eggs lightly in a large bowl, Crumble in the feta cheese and stir in the scallions and spinach. Season with the mint and black pepper.

2. Defrost the phyllo according to the package directions.

3. Preheat the oven to 350 degrees F.

4. Remove the dough from the box, unroll it and place flat on your work surface, covering with a cloth or plastic wrap to keep it from drying out. Take off one sheet and re-cover the pile. Use a pizza cutter to cut the sheet in half the long way, creating two strips 6 x 16 inches each. Brush one half of each with melted butter and fold over the long way, making two strips 3 x 16 inches. Butter the tops of each.

5. Place 1 tablespoon of the filling at the bottom of each strip. Fold over the filling to create a triangle, then continue folding (like a flag) all the way up the strip. Repeat with the second strip. Place on a buttered baking tray and butter the tops. Repeat with the other sheets of phyllo.

You can cut the recipe in half or freeze some of them to be baked later. There is no need to defrost. Bake for 30 to 35 minutes or until they are golden brown and crispy.

Pohaça *(poh-ah-cha)*

Makes about 30

Contributed by
Sevil Bostanci Aktas

Sevil: This is a great example of Turkish baking: a savory treat with white cheese and parsley. I remember, when I was a child, my mom, my sister and I made peynirli pogaça and other delicious foods together, especially at weekends. Turkish people love making and eating baked goods. We make this for getting together days — for example, religious festivals, holidays, etc. There are lots of styles of pohaças. This one is made with yeast and is fluffy. Another one is with baking powder; it is more crispy and crusty. Pohaça can be stuffed with potatoes, olives, ground beef, or cheese, and have grains and herbs like sesame, black sesame or dried dill in the dough or sprinkled on top.

INGREDIENTS

DOUGH:

2 tablespoons yeast

1½ cups lukewarm whole milk

1½ cups yogurt whey, prepared ahead *

2 cups olive oil

¼ cup lukewarm water

1 egg, plus 2 egg whites (yolks will go into topping glaze)

12 cups flour

1 teaspoon salt

3 teaspoons sugar

FILLING:

2 cups crumbled feta cheese

½ cup shredded mozzarella cheese

⅔ cup fresh parsley, finely chopped

2 teaspoons red pepper flakes

STEPS

1. Preheat the oven to 375 degrees F.

2. *For the dough:* Combine all the liquids, salt and sugar in a big bowl and mix well and add half of flour. Continue to mix. Add the rest of the flour. Knead well with your hands (or machine) for a few minutes, until the dough comes together. Shape the dough like a ball, place it in the bowl and cover it. (I prepare dough at night and put it in the refrigerator. In the morning take it out and wait until it has doubled in size.)

3. *For the filling:* In a medium-size bowl, stir in the crumbled feta cheese, chopped parsley and pepper, and mix well. Once the dough has risen, punch down and divide into 28 to 30 equal pieces. Roll each piece into a ball, and then flatten into a round flat circle with your fingertips.

4. Place a spoonful of the filling mixture onto each round (take care not to overfill), fold two opposite edges up and bring together. Place the stuffed dough on a rimmed baking sheet and continue this procedure with the rest of the dough pieces. Cover with another baking sheet or wax paper or a kitchen towel and let rest for 30 minutes.

2 beaten egg yolks (whites were for the dough)

Sesame seeds and nigella seeds (nigella optional if unavailable)

5. Brush each pohaça with the beaten egg yolks and sprinkle with sesame seeds and/or nigella. Bake on the middle rack for about 20 to 25 minutes, until they are golden brown at top.

* *Liquid whey:* Line a large strainer with an unbleached cheesecloth or thin, clean dish towel and set strainer in large bowl. Pour yogurt or kefir into the cloth, cover and allow to sit out at room temperature for several hours. The liquid whey will begin to drip into the bowl, while the milk solids will stay collected in the cloth.

Just one piece of pohaça is enough to fill you. You can make smaller pieces if you like. I always make more and put in the freezer and enjoy anytime I want. It is a life saver, especially when you are on the road for a trip or want a treat for unexpected guests. Simply take out of the freezer, heat 30 seconds in the microwave and it's ready to enjoy!

Delicious cheesy pogaça is a favorite affordable breakfast or tea time treat in Turkey. You can find it in any bakery or in street stalls, and it is so easy to make at home. Make your kitchen smell heavenly, invite a friend and treat with a glass of cay (tea).

Asparagus With Goat Cheese In Phyllo

About 6 servings

Here's another way to use that phyllo dough. These little packages look so fancy that you can use them as appetizers or even as a first course.

INGREDIENTS

24 asparagus spears

4 ounces goat cheese

1–2 tablespoons milk or cream

½ pound phyllo dough

1 stick melted butter

STEPS

1. Preheat the oven to 375 degrees F.

2. Cut the asparagus to a uniform length of about 4 inches. (Save the ends for asparagus soup or omelets.) If the stalks are thick you might want to use a potato peeler to trim the tough skin from the bottom half.

3. Mix the goat cheese with enough milk or cream to soften it to the consistency of cake frosting. Put the cheese into a piping bag with a very thin tip or use a zipper bag with one of the bottom corners snipped.

4. Cut 14 x 18-inch phyllo dough in half crosswise, giving you 2 rectangles, 14 x 9 inches each. Put half in the refrigerator for a future use and keep the other half on your work table covered in plastic wrap. Take one sheet at a time and brush it completely with melted butter. Put an asparagus spear at one end. Pipe a thin bead of the cheese along the length of the asparagus. Fold the sides in and roll up into a tight tube. Place in a buttered baking pan and brush the top with more butter. Continue until all the asparagus are rolled. Bake until they are deep golden brown.

Baked Brie

When my girls were growing up I wanted to make the New Year's Eve celebrations special for them and then when they got older I encouraged them to invite their friends to our house. I told them they could have any snacks they wanted. I have to admit that one of their favorites was aerosol cheese. They would spray it on crackers, their fingers and sometimes directly into their mouths. Times and tastes have changed. Now I think they would definitely prefer this soft cheese preparation.

INGREDIENTS

1 (8-ounce) brie wheel

1 sheet puff pastry

4 tablespoons orange marmalade

4 tablespoons toasted sliced almonds

1 egg, beaten

STEPS

1. Preheat the oven to 350 degrees F.

2. Lay out the pastry sheet on a lightly floured board. Roll and trim the sheet until it measures approximately 10 x 10 inches. Place the marmalade in the center of the square. Sprinkle the almonds on top.

3. Carefully place the wheel of brie on top of the almonds. Fold up the corners and sides and pinch together to seal completely. Trim excess pastry. Turn the package seam side down on a baking sheet which has been covered with parchment paper or aluminum foil.

4. Roll out the extra pastry and use decorative cutters to make leaves or other shapes. Brush the top and sides with the beaten egg and place the decorative pieces on top. Brush again with the beaten egg. Bake until the pastry has puffed and turned golden, approximately 30 minutes. Let cool a few minutes before serving.

Variations: Try these combinations: apricot jam and toasted hazelnuts, or raspberry jam and walnuts.

Stuffed French Toast

8 servings

When my niece Laura got married, they had the ceremony in Chapel Hill, North Carolina, and it was there that I was introduced to the Carolina Diner, a college hangout and purveyor of decadent comfort foods. One of their specialties was French Toast that was coated in crushed Frosted Flakes. I decided to go them one better by stuffing two pieces of bread with cream cheese and preserves and then coating them with crushed cereal and frying them in butter until the outside was crunchy and inside was gooey.

INGREDIENTS

6 eggs

1 cup cream

1 teaspoon cinnamon

1 teaspoon vanilla

1 tablespoon sugar

⅛ teaspoon salt

16 slices egg bread

16 ounces cream cheese

8 ounces fruit preserves (blueberry, strawberry, etc.)

4 cups corn flakes, crushed

2 tablespoons butter

STEPS

1. Beat the eggs with the cream, cinnamon, vanilla, sugar and salt. Spread eight of the bread slices with cream cheese and the other eight with preserves. Put them together and dip the sandwiches into the batter to coat lightly. Then dip them in the crushed corn flakes.

2. Melt the butter in a skillet or griddle over medium heat and fry the sandwiches until they are golden brown on both sides. Add more butter to the pan as needed. Remove the finished toast to a platter in a warm oven or chafing dish. Sprinkle with confectioner's sugar, if desired, and serve with maple syrup or fruit sauce.

Arepas

Makes 10

Contributed by

Alberto Benzaquen

This recipe comes from Alberto Benzaquen, a passionate devotee of arepas. He is willing to admit that it is a dish made throughout Latin America but he is adamant that the one true version comes from Venezuela:

Alberto: The arepa is a Pre-Columbian dish from the area that is now Colombia and Venezuela. Instruments used to make flour for the arepas, and the clay slabs on which they were cooked, were often found at archaeological sites in the area. Although it has not been specified in which country an arepa was cooked for the first time, it has been possible to define the oldest dates of the presence of maize(corn) in Colombia and in Venezuela.

Throughout its history, the arepa has stayed mainly unchanged from the arepas that pre-Columbian native peoples would have consumed,

INGREDIENTS

BASIC DOUGH:

2½ cups water, warm

2 cups P.A.N. (Harina P.A.N.)

1 teaspoon salt

FILLING VARIATIONS:

1. Reyna Pe'piaa (Reina Pepiada):

   2 chicken breasts

   1 ripe Hass avocado, peeled, pitted, and coarsely chopped

   ¼ cup mayonnaise

   3 tablespoons minced fresh cilantro

   Salt, pepper

   Optional: **diced yellow onions to taste**

2. Cheese (Cheese of your choice):

   Venezuelan cheeses are not always available, but you can use Gouda, queso fresco or queso cotija.

*Harina P.A.N. is pre-cooked white corn meal. It is NOT the same as the masa harina used in Mexico for gorditas or tortillas. Harina P.A.N. is readily available online.

3. Capressa:

   5 tomatoes (sliced), a slice of mozzarella cheese and a basil leaf per arepa, olive oil, salt and pepper to taste.

4. Seafood "Vuelve a la vida":

   Seafood of your choice, simmered in tomato sauce. Add crushed red pepper to make it *arrabiata* style.

making the arepa one of the few pre-contact traditions that have remained popular in the years since colonization.

The word arepa may have originated from the language of the Caracas natives, on the north coast of Venezuela that meant maize (corn). It is a ground maize dough or pre-cooked flour prominent in the cuisine of Colombia and Venezuela, and today there is one difference between them: The Venezuelan arepas are "stuffed," Colombian are not!

For our family, an arepa is the daily bread of Venezuela handed down through generations from the "Timoto-Cuicas," a local tribe, to our families today. The dough is formed into a patty, grilled on a budare, baked, split open and "stuffed" with a variety of ingredients, like a sandwich. They are naturally gluten-free and take the place of bread in most Venezuelan homes.

STEPS

1. *For the dough:* Pour water into a bowl. Add the salt and corn meal gradually. Knead until a smooth dough is formed and let rest for 3 to 5 minutes. Separate dough into 10 portions. Take one portion in your hands and shape it into a ball, then press it with your palms to form a large patty shape of about 3 ½ inches in diameter. Place onto the griddle (budare) or frying pan over medium heat for about 5 minutes on each side. Brown on both sides and serve hot. Open the arepa and stuff it with your favorite fillings.

2. *For the filling:* Place the chicken breasts in a medium saucepan and add water to cover by 2 inches. Add 1/2 teaspoon salt and bring to a simmer over medium heat, uncovered until the chicken is cooked through for about 15 minutes. Remove chicken from the sauce pan and let cool completely. Tear the chicken into shreds.

3. Mash the avocados with a large fork until smooth, add the mayonnaise, and stir in the cilantro. Add the chicken. Season with salt and pepper. Cover and refrigerate until ready to serve.

Mandaue Empanada

Makes 14

Contributed by
Luella Ouano McClernan

Luella: My family is originally from the coastal town of Mandaue in the island of Cebu. This is the central region of the Philippines called the Visayas. Our cuisine is different from that of the northern and southern regions.

More than three hundred years of Spanish rule has greatly influenced our cuisine as well as our traditions. As a child, my favorite time of the day was "merienda" with my siblings. We had light snacks between 3pm and 4pm. My favorite food back then was empanada, which is definitely of Spanish origin.

When I came to America, I realized how much I missed the home-cooked foods my mom made. The only problem was she never wrote down the recipes. When our family has get-together parties, we usually feast on Filipino food.

(continued on page 108)

INGREDIENTS

FILLING:

2 tablespoons canola oil

2 cloves of garlic minced

¼ cup chopped sweet onion

½ pound ground pork

¼ cup finely diced potatoes

¼ cup finely diced carrots

¼ cup water

¼ cup frozen baby sweet peas

½ cup raisins

2 teaspoons oyster sauce with no MSG

Salt and black pepper to taste

STEPS

1. *For the filling:* Sauté garlic and onion in non-stick pan with the canola oil. Add ground pork and sauté until no longer pink. Add potato, carrot and water. Cover and cook until soft. Add peas and raisins. Season with oyster sauce, salt and pepper to taste. Stir and cook covered on low heat. Put in a strainer and allow filling to cool.

(continued on page 108)

Mandaue Empanada *(continued)*

Over the years, my Aunt Pat has gained a reputation for making the best empanadas and other island delicacies. She has tried many dough recipes but she made her empanada better by using my Aunt Honey's pastry recipe. Her crispy, flaky pastry with blisters on its surface is what made her empanada exceptional. There is a hint of sweetness to Filipino empanada. Some cooks add more sugar to the dough and filling.

Empanada tastes best when fried but can also be baked. The filling may be different depending on individual or family preferences.

INGREDIENTS

DOUGH:

2 cups flour

½ teaspoon salt

1½ tablespoons sugar

2 tablespoons butter

3 tablespoons canola oil

1 large beaten egg

10 tablespoons cold water

Canola oil for deep-frying

ADDITIONAL FILLING:

½ cup shredded sharp Cheddar cheese

1 hard-boiled egg thinly sliced lengthwise

STEPS

2. *For the dough:* Mix flour with salt and sugar. Add butter and mix. Add oil and mix again. Add beaten egg, mix, then add water, 2 tablespoons at a time. Work dough with hands after each 2 tablespoons are added. Keep adding water until dough is no longer crumbly and holds together. Gather into a ball. Cover with plastic wrap and allow dough to rest for 15 minutes. Flatten ball and divide into 12 equal wedges. Make small balls out of dough wedges. Keep dough covered with plastic wrap.

3. Flatten each ball and roll out into a thin disk using a rolling pin. Use dusting of flour to prevent sticking. Put 1 tablespoon of filling at center of imperfect disk. Top with cheese and a slice of egg. Wet edge with water using fingers. Fold dough in half over filling. Pick up edges and pinch all around to secure filling.

4. Lay filled dough on board and trim off excess dough around edge with knife, allowing 1/2 inch for crimping. Press down again around edge before crimping. Lift edge with index finger and fold in corner of filled dough to form a small triangle then press down against board to seal edge. Continue folding in dough triangles along entire edge and pressing down each time to seal. Small dough triangles created actually overlap to form a braided edge. This crimping technique is called *repulgue*.

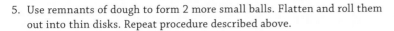
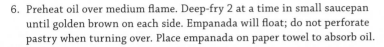

5. Use remnants of dough to form 2 more small balls. Flatten and roll them out into thin disks. Repeat procedure described above.

6. Preheat oil over medium flame. Deep-fry 2 at a time in small saucepan until golden brown on each side. Empanada will float; do not perforate pastry when turning over. Place empanada on paper towel to absorb oil.

Lamí kaayo! (Very delicious!)

Black Bean Quesadillas

Makes 4

Mexican cuisine is a treasure trove of stuffed foods. Think tacos, tamales, burritos, empanadas and quesadillas. And every recipe has a hundred variations based on available ingredients and food preferences. We often make chicken and cheese quesadillas when we end up with leftover rotisserie chicken. The technique is all the same.

INGREDIENTS

FILLING:

1 tablespoon vegetable oil

1 medium onion, chopped

1 clove garlic, minced

1 red pepper, diced

1 cup frozen corn

1 (15-ounce) can black beans, rinsed and drained

1 tablespoon chili powder

Salt

8 soft 10- or 12-inch flour tortillas

8 ounces shredded cheese (Cheddar, Monterey Jack, etc.)

4 small pats of butter

STEPS

1. *For the filling:* Heat the oil in a large skillet over medium high heat. Add the onion and stir until soft. Add the garlic, diced red peppers, corn and beans. Stir until heated through and then season with chili powder and salt to taste. Take the mixture off the heat.

2. Sprinkle one tortilla with some cheese and top with about a cup of the filling. Spread the filling to within an inch of the edge. Top with another sprinkling of cheese and a second tortilla.

3. In another skillet, melt a pat of butter and gently place the stacked tortillas in the pan. Press down lightly with a large spatula and cook until golden brown. Carefully flip the quesadilla to brown on the other side.

4. Press down lightly and use the spatula to remove the quesadilla to a baking tray that you can keep in a warming oven while you cook the other quesadillas. Use a sharp knife or pizza cutter to cut the circles into wedges. Serve with salsa, pico di gallo, guacamole and sour cream.

Cornish Pasties

Makes 6

If you pronounce the name of this dish the way it looks, it doesn't sound very appetizing... like the pasties might literally stick to your ribs, But I'm told the proper name for this dish is Pass-tees. And that's what I'm going to call them. In any case, they are one of those delicious hand-held foods just perfect for a picnic or a lunchbox.

INGREDIENTS

DOUGH:

3 cups flour

½ teaspoon salt

½ cup vegetable shortening (Crisco)

1 egg

2 teaspoons apple cider vinegar

3 tablespoons water

FILLING:

1 pound diced beef, raw

½ cup each diced onion and rutabaga

1 cup diced potatoes

½ cup frozen peas

2 sprigs fresh thyme

2 tablespoons Worcestershire sauce

Salt and pepper

1 egg, beaten (for egg wash)

STEPS

1. *For the dough:* Place all the pastry ingredients except the water in the bowl of a food processor. Pulse a few times to cut in the shortening. Then continue to pulse as you add the water until a dough forms and cleans the side of the bowl. Remove and knead on a floured board for a few turns until completely smooth. Divide the dough into 6 pieces and form into disks. Cover each with plastic wrap and let rest for at least 20 minutes.

2. Mix all the filling ingredients in a bowl.

3. Preheat the oven to 400 degrees F.

4. Roll out each disk on a floured board into an 8-inch circle. Fill with 1/6th of the mixture, fold over and seal. Turn the packet so that the edge is facing up. Crimp as you would for a pie crust and turn the ends up slightly to form the traditional pastie.

5. Place the finished pasties on a baking sheet and brush with the egg wash. Bake for 20 to 30 minutes until the crust is golden brown and the interior registers at least 150 degrees F.

Vegetarian option: It's easy to eliminate the meat from this recipe and substitute more root vegetables such as carrots, turnips and parsnips.

Arancini

Makes 4

In Italian, the word means "little oranges," and that is what they resemble with their golden colored toasted breadcrumb exterior. Hiding inside is the creamy texture of rice with egg and cheese and finally the tangy filling with North African-inspired spices. We call it the perfect food because it is delicious hot or cold, with milk, beer, wine or coffee. The Roman versions are called "suppli" and they usually have tomato sauce mixed in with the rice. But beware! These tasty mouthfuls are both addictive and extremely time consuming. It takes about five times as long to make one as to eat one.

INGREDIENTS

¼ pound chopped beef

1 small onion finely chopped

3 tablespoons tomato puree

1 tablespoon pecorino Romano cheese

¼ teaspoon ground cloves

¼ teaspoon nutmeg

2 tablespoons white wine

Salt and pepper

½ cup shredded mozzarella

RICE MIXTURE:

2 cups rice

1 tablespoon butter

1 teaspoon salt

1 stick butter, melted

8 eggs, separated and beaten

½ cup pecorino Romano cheese

2 cups plain breadcrumbs

STEPS

1. Sauté the chopped beef and onion until the meat is brown and the onion is soft. Add the next 6 ingredients and set aside to cool, and then add the shredded mozzarella.

2. Cook the rice in 4 cups of water with the tablespoon of butter and the salt. Add the stick of melted butter, egg yolks and grated cheese. Let it cool and then rest for 1 hour in the refrigerator.

3. Heat oil in a deep fryer or heat 1 inch of fat in a deep skillet. Place about 1/2 cup of the rice mixture in the bottom of a ladle. Spread it out and then top with about 1 tablespoon of the meat mixture. Top with another 1/2 cup of the rice. Scoop out the ball and round it gently in your hands. Roll in the beaten egg whites and then the breadcrumbs.

4. Place a few of the balls in the deep fryer or the skillet and cook until deep golden brown. Drain on paper towels.

Zeppoli With Anchovy

Makes about 12

Zeppoli are most often served as a sweet treat covered in powdered sugar, the Italian version of fried dough. But this version uses a similar dough to create a savory version filled with just a taste of salty anchovies and some melty mozzarella. They don't hold up well so plan to eat these as soon as they come out of the fryer.

INGREDIENTS

DOUGH:

2 teaspoons yeast (one packet)

1 tablespoon sugar

1½ cups lukewarm water

3 tablespoons olive oil

3 cups flour

1 teaspoon salt

Canola oil for frying

1 can rolled salted anchovy fillets

8 ounces mozzarella, cut in ½-inch cubes

STEPS

1. Dissolve the yeast and sugar in the lukewarm water. Add the olive oil and let rest for 10 minutes to let the yeast proof.

2. Combine the flour and salt in the bowl of a mixer fitted with the dough hook. Add the yeast mixture and knead for 8 minutes. It should be more like a sticky batter than a firm dough. Cover the bowl and let it rest for 1 hour.

3. Heat the oil in a saucepan to 340 degrees F. Scoop out 2 tablespoons of the dough. Stick an anchovy and a cube of cheese in the middle and pull the dough around it. Drop into the hot oil and fry until puffed and golden brown. Drain on a rack and let cool slightly before serving.

PART FOUR

SEAFOOD & MEATS

So far, we've been talking about recipes that involve stuffing ingredients like meats, cheeses and vegetables into bread or dough. But sometimes the tables are turned. Stuffing meat and seafood with a variety of flavored fillings, creates memorable dishes where the sum is much greater than the individual parts.

This is also an area where you can really let your creative juices flow. We all know how many variations there are for something as simple as turkey stuffing. Let your imagination run wild on these recipes. You can also cater the ingredients to the picky eaters in your house. No mushrooms? Fine. No garlic? Fine. There are always fun things to substitute.

Scotch Eggs

6 servings

If you ever have a chance to visit London, don't miss the opportunity to wander the aisles of Fortnum & Mason. The architecture of the building itself is fascinating and it is like a living museum of all things truly British. This is especially true in the downstairs food court where, in addition to a mind boggling assortment of teas from around the world, you can sample every kind of English food specialty from bangers and mushy peas to meat pies and Scotch eggs. They actually claim to have invented this savory treat near the end of the eighteenth century but the name came from Londoners who noticed that the officers of the Scots Guards, who had their barracks around Wellington Station, had a particular affection for the snack.

INGREDIENTS

12 ounces bulk spicy sausage meat

1 teaspoon chopped fresh thyme

1 teaspoon fresh chopped rosemary

⅓ cup breadcrumbs

6 hard boiled eggs, shelled

1 egg, lightly beaten

STEPS

1. Preheat the oven to 400 degrees F.

2. Mix together the sausage meat, thyme and rosemary. Divide the meat into 6 portions, 2 ounces each.

3. Sprinkle a few breadcrumbs on the work surface. Pat a sausage meat portion into a 2½-inch circle. Wrap it around a hard boiled egg, completely covering it. Make sure the egg is not showing. Dip in the beaten egg then roll in the breadcrumbs.

4. Prepare all the eggs in the same manner. Place them on a baking sheet. Bake until golden brown, about 20 minutes. Cool slightly before serving. Cut in half or quarters to serve. If desired, serve with mustard.

Note: An alternate way to cook these is on top of the stove in 2 to 3 inches of oil.

Deviled Eggs

Makes 24 stuffed halves

Before eggs got a bad reputation in the dietary world, we seemed to eat them morning noon and night. We even had an eggman, Roy, who delivered fresh eggs to our house in Brooklyn. We had them fried and scrambled and soft boiled for breakfast, in frittatas for lunch and dinner and in any number of baked goods. And then there were the parties where platters of deviled eggs bedecked every table and people shared their latest combination of condiments used to "devil" their egg recipes. The filling in this recipe is pretty straightforward but the presentation elevates it to a show stopper for your next picnic or potluck.

INGREDIENTS

1 dozen eggs

Two cups leftover ham, diced

1 small onion, diced

1 tablespoon mustard

1 tablespoon hot sauce (Franks, Crystal, etc.)

4 tablespoons mayonnaise, or more

Salt and pepper to taste

Paprika

¼ pound bacon

2 tablespoons cider vinegar

Salt and pepper

4 cups baby spinach leaves

½ cup grated carrot

STEPS

1. *To hard-boil:* Put the uncooked eggs in a saucepan large enough to cover them with water. Bring to a boil, then cover and take off the heat. Allow to sit for 10 minutes. Drain and chill the eggs with ice water.

2. Peel the eggs and cut in half lengthwise. Remove the yolks to a large mixing bowl. In a food processor, chop the ham and onion until fine. Add to the yolks. Mix in the mustard, hot sauce and mayonnaise, salt and pepper and mix well. Add more mayonnaise if necessary to moisten. Fill the egg whites with the mixture and sprinkle with a dusting of paprika.

3. Cook the bacon until crisp and drain on paper towels. Save about 2 tablespoons of the rendered bacon grease to whisk in a bowl with the vinegar, salt and pepper.

4. Spread the spinach leaves on a large platter and drizzle with the bacon dressing. Place the deviled eggs on top and sprinkle the platter with the grated carrot and crumbled bacon. If there are deviled eggs left, you can simply chop them up and use as an egg salad spread for lunchbox sandwiches.

Rouladen

6 servings

My mother's cousin Steve met and fell in love with a young German girl while he was stationed over there after World War II. We kids all thought that Rosemary was the most beautiful woman we had ever seen. She showered us all with affection and became an integral part of every family function. She and Steve became godparents to my younger brother, Joseph. Rosemary loved my mother's Italian specialties but as I got older and more interested in different foods, I wanted her to show me the way to authentic German dishes like kartoffelpfannkuchen and rouladen. She was happy to oblige.

INGREDIENTS

6 slices beef round

2 tablespoons good mustard

6 slices bacon

6 spears dill pickle

1 cup sauerkraut, rinsed and drained

½ cup flour

Salt and pepper to taste

2 tablespoons vegetable oil

STEPS

1. Have the butcher cut the slices approximately 1/8-inch thick. If the slices are too thick, you'll need to pound them out to be able to roll them properly.

2. Spread a teaspoon of mustard on each slice along with a slice of bacon, a pickle spear, and a tablespoon or so of sauerkraut. Roll the meat over the stuffing, tuck in the ends and continue to roll up into a bundle. Secure with kitchen twine or toothpicks. Dredge the rolls in flour that has been seasoned with pepper and a little salt. Go easy on the salt since the bacon, pickle and kraut will add plenty of saltiness.

3. Heat the oil in a large Dutch oven and brown the rolls on all sides. Add enough boiling water to barely cover the rolls. Bring to a boil then reduce to a simmer. Cover and cook for 2 hours.

Stuffed Flank Steak

4 servings

This is another recipe from our dear friend and Kitchen Magician, Joe Certo. Although he is a practicing oral surgeon, he is also a trained chef and culinary instructor. He has lent his expertise to our public television cooking shows for twenty-five years and often came out in front of the camera as well to share some of his favorite recipes. This one takes a rather humble cut of meat and elevates it to a centerpiece for a company dinner.

INGREDIENTS

1 to 1½-pound flank steak

FILLING:

1 small can mushrooms (or fresh if available)

1 onion, diced

1½ cup melted butter or margarine

4–5 slices bread

½ cup pecorino Romano cheese, grated

½ cup chopped walnuts

1 egg

Salt and pepper to taste

STEPS

1. Preheat the oven to 375 degrees F.

2. Cut pocket in one side of flank steak.

3. *For the filling:* Add mushrooms and diced onions to melted butter or margarine, and sauté until onions are transparent. In a bowl combine bread, cheese, nuts, eggs, and slowly add margarine/butter mixture. Add salt and pepper to taste.

4. Place stuffing into pocket of flank steak and close with toothpick. Bake for at least 30 minutes or until desired doneness. Slice the flank steak into 1½-inch slices.

Stuffed Flounder

4 servings

When I moved to Pittsburgh almost thirty-five years ago, my one reason for concern was that the city was so far away from salt water. The people at WQED were smart enough to take me to the Strip District as the first step in my orientation. One visit to Benkovitz Seafoods on a Saturday morning was sufficient proof that proximity to the ocean was not a prerequisite for a love of seafood. The place was jammed with people slurping steamy cups of seafood bisque while they waited in line for fried fish sandwiches. Behind the fresh seafood counter were mounds of shrimp, mussels, whole fish and a variety of fillets. Then I found Wholey's! They also serve prepared fish, jumbo portions freshly fried or broiled. They've recently added a sushi bar and huge tanks filled with trout, bass and carp from which you can select your supper. This city is a seafood haven!

INGREDIENTS

FILLING:

1 cup breadcrumbs

2 tablespoons olive oil

Juice of 1 lemon

½ teaspoon oregano

Salt and pepper

2 tablespoons chopped parsley

1 tablespoon capers

1 tablespoon toasted pine nuts

4 small flounder fillets

2 tablespoons melted butter

¼ cup dry white wine, approx.

STEPS

1. Preheat the oven to 325 degrees F.

2. *For the filling:* Combine the breadcrumbs with the other filling ingredients. The mixture should be moist so add a few extra drops of oil if necessary.

3. Rinse the fish and spread the tops of each fillet with the filling. Carefully roll up each fillet from one end, tucking in the sides as you go. Secure with a toothpick and place in a small, buttered baking dish. Brush each roll-up with a little melted butter or olive oil.

4. Put about 1/4 cup of white wine in the dish and bake 20 to 30 minutes. This is great served with some sautéed spinach, white rice and the rest of the bottle of wine you used for cooking.

Stuffed Trout En Croûte

4 servings

It never seems to fail that I'm sitting in a restaurant with something simple like a pork chop on my plate and one of the servers walks by carrying a dish that looks and smells absolutely terrific. You want to stop them in mid-stride and say, "Where the heck was that on the menu?!?"

Many years ago I found myself in a very classy little French restaurant called "Jour et Nuit" in the Georgetown section of Washington, D.C. It was the kind of place where congressmen might steal away for a civilized meal and foreign diplomats frequented for a taste of authentic continental cuisine. On the menu was a simple description for stuffed trout in pastry crust. Since so many of the other entrees involved ingredients with which I was unfamiliar at the time (and still have no particular fondness for), I opted for the fish.

INGREDIENTS

2 trout, dressed and boned

1⅓ packages puff pastry

¼ pound bay scallops

¼ pound small shrimp, peeled and deveined

2–3 tablespoons cream

8 asparagus spears

Salt and pepper

1 egg beaten with 1 tablespoon water

SAUCE:

2 tablespoons butter

2 tablespoons flour

1 cup white wine

1 cup fish stock or clam juice

2 tablespoons lemon juice

Salt and pepper

1 teaspoon cracked coriander

STEPS

1. Preheat the oven to 375 degrees F and line a baking pan with parchment paper.

2. Rinse and pat dry the trout. Follow package directions to thaw the puff pastry. Roll each of the four pastry pieces on a lightly floured board until it is larger than the fish.

3. In the bowl of a food processor, pulse the scallops and shrimp. With the machine turned on, slowly add the heavy cream until a smooth mousseline is formed. It should be smooth but thick enough to hold its shape on a spoon.

4. Trim, wash and dry the asparagus and peel the tough outer skin from the bottoms. Lay a fish on one of the sheets of puff pastry. Season with salt and pepper. Put about 1/2 cup of the scallop/shrimp mixture inside the fish. Layer four of the asparagus spears along the length of the fish and cover with more of the scallop/shrimp. Cover with a second piece of puff pastry. Wet the edges with pastry brush and seal. Press the pastry close to the outline of the trout and trim, but accentuate the shape of the tail and upper fin. Use the scraps to decorate the top with fish features like gills or scales or fins.

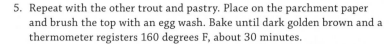

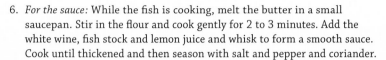

5. Repeat with the other trout and pastry. Place on the parchment paper and brush the top with an egg wash. Bake until dark golden brown and a thermometer registers 160 degrees F, about 30 minutes.

6. *For the sauce:* While the fish is cooking, melt the butter in a small saucepan. Stir in the flour and cook gently for 2 to 3 minutes. Add the white wine, fish stock and lemon juice and whisk to form a smooth sauce. Cook until thickened and then season with salt and pepper and coriander.

What arrived was a platter adorned with a golden fish fashioned from pastry. Inside the sculpture was a completely boned trout stuffed with a mixture of shrimp and scallops. Everyone looked at my dish as it made its way from the kitchen to the table.

Now, almost thirty years later, I've seen enough episodes of Jacques Pepin and Julia Child to try and duplicate this fabulous dish.

Stuffed Clams

Makes about 12 half-shells

It's not always easy to get fresh clams for this recipe but you can always get canned or jarred chopped clams. For that reason, I save a few dozen clamshells and just run them through the dishwasher cycle. Once they are dry you can just store them in a plastic zip bag for the next time you get the urge for stuffed clams.

INGREDIENTS

12 large clams (cohogs)

2 cups breadcrumbs

Juice of 2–3 lemons, approx. ⅓ cup

3 tablespoons olive oil

2 teaspoon oregano

Salt and pepper to taste

STEPS

1. Preheat the oven to 350 degrees F.

2. When buying clams, make sure they are closed and as fresh as possible. Throw clams into boiling water just until they open. Remove clam from shell and clean clams, removing and disposing of black sack. Drain and reserve clam juice. Chop up clam meat.

3. Mix together breadcrumbs, lemon juice, olive oil, oregano, salt and pepper. Mix with clams and stuff shells. Pour reserved juice over clams to moisten. Place in baking dish and bake until breadcrumbs brown on top.

Hint: To make sure clams are fresh, put them in a pot of water. If they float, discard them. To make them less sandy, sprinkle cornmeal over them and cover with water. Soon afterwards the clams will dispel most of their sand.

Calamari

3 servings as a main dish, 4 or so servings as a side dish

Every year on Christmas Eve, my mother and grandmother would put together a feast of seafood. In the old church rubrics it was a day of abstinence, meaning no meat. But it was a feast nonetheless with clam sauce for linguini, shrimp oreganato, flounder roll-ups, and calamari or squid. Gram would spend an hour at the sink cleaning the calamari to within an inch of its life. Fortunately, you can now buy the calamari already cleaned into neat white tubes. The rule with calamari is to cook it short or long; in between will be tough and rubbery.

INGREDIENTS

FILLING:

2 tablespoons olive oil

1 onion, finely chopped

1 clove garlic, minced

½ cup breadcrumbs

1 teaspoon red pepper flakes (optional)

¼ cup grated pecorino Romano cheese

4 tablespoons chopped fresh parsley

1 (4-ounce) can small shrimp, drained

Salt and pepper

1 egg

6 cleaned calamari tubes

2 tablespoons olive oil

½ cup white wine

1 cup grape tomatoes, cut in half

STEPS

1. Heat the oil in a small frying pan and sauté the onion until soft but not brown. Add the minced garlic and stir for just a minute.

2. In a mixing bowl, combine the breadcrumbs, red pepper flakes, cheese, parsley, shrimp, salt and pepper. When the onions and garlic are cooled add them to the bowl with the egg and mix well. Fill each calamari tube with some of the stuffing. Don't pack them too tightly. The filling will expand and the calamari will shrink during cooking. Secure the ends of the tubes with toothpick.

3. Heat the olive oil in a covered sauté pan. Put the stuffed calamari in the hot oil to sear on all sides. Add the white wine and cook until almost evaporated. Add the tomatoes and cook over high heat until they begin to simmer. Cover and reduce the heat to low. Simmer for about another 30 minutes.

The sauce created by the tomatoes will have a delicious seafood flavor, so I like to serve this with some pasta to soak up all that flavor.

Chicken Brione

8 servings

In 1965 I applied for a summer
job in the band at a resort in
the Catskills. I told them I was
a drummer. What I didn't reveal
was that I had never actually
played the drums. I had been
assistant timpanist in the high
school band and shook the
maracas or tinkled the triangle.
Fortunately, they had already
hired the band but they were
in desperate need of a waiter.
I had never done that either
so I felt just as qualified. The
dining room seated 125 and I
was the only waiter. The salary
was $20 per week plus tips,
which were ceremoniously
conferred in sealed envelopes
at the end of the week by
the matriarch or patriarch of
the family.

INGREDIENTS

1 cup breadcrumbs

½ teaspoon oregano

½ teaspoon parsley

¼ cup pecorino Romano
   cheese

Dash garlic powder

2 lemons

8 boneless chicken cutlets

8 slices of prosciutto

½ pound mozzarella

4 tablespoons butter

1 cup dry white wine
   (Soave or Pino Grigio)

1 cup chicken stock

Salt and pepper

STEPS

1. Mix the breadcrumbs with the spices,
   grated cheese and the juice of one lemon.
   Pound the cutlets between plastic sheets
   until they are 1/4-inch thick. On each
   cutlet place a piece of prosciutto, 2 or 3
   tablespoons of the breadcrumbs mixture
   and a strip of mozzarella. Roll halfway,
   then tuck in the sides and continue
   rolling to make a neat bundle. Secure
   with a toothpick.

2. Melt the butter in a large skillet and
   quickly brown the chicken rolls. Remove
   them to a warm platter and deglaze the
   pan with the wine. Add the chicken stock
   and the juice of the other lemon. Season
   with salt and pepper and return the
   chicken to the pan. Reduce to a simmer,
   cover the pan and let cook gently for
   20 minutes.

They were from the city of Trieste. The owner and his wife ran the hotel portion while his father cooked all the food and his mother helped with preparation. I only made a few hundred dollars that summer but in retrospect I should have paid them for all I learned about hard work, human nature and fabulous food.

One of the chef's signature dishes was a boned chicken that he stuffed, rolled and sautéed in a white wine and lemon sauce. Chef Vosilla could bone a chicken down to the wing tips in about one minute. In the interest of convenience I have adapted the recipe to use chicken cutlets.

Chicken Kiev

4 servings

I worked at WNET in New York for thirteen years. One of the great perks was that we were located on 58th Street near 8th Avenue. Within a few blocks of our office were some of the finest and most famous restaurants, places like Patsy's, Asia Numero Uno and The Russian Tea Room. The latter, nestled beside Carnegie Hall on 57th Street, was like being on a movie set, the waiters dressed as Cossacks, balancing trays of food and drinks while they danced their way between tables. It was the place to see and be seen in the entertainment world. And, the food was fabulous. There I had my first taste of blini with caviar, borscht, and the classic chicken Kiev, oozing out its center of molten butter as you cut it on your plate.

INGREDIENTS

1 stick (4 ounces) softened butter

1 tablespoon fresh chopped parsley

1 tablespoon fresh chopped chives

4 boneless, skinless chicken breasts

1 egg beaten with 1 tablespoon milk

1 cup plain breadcrumbs

Oil for frying

Salt and pepper to taste

STEPS

1. Mix the soft butter with the fresh herbs. Spread onto plastic wrap and roll into a cylinder. Freeze until firm. Meanwhile, pound each chicken breast between plastic wrap until 1/4-inch thick or less.

2. Divide the butter into four pieces. Place each piece on a chicken breast and roll up, tucking in the sides. Secure the end with a toothpick. Dip each roll into the egg mixture and then coat with breadcrumbs. Return to the refrigerator for at least 30 minutes.

3. Heat the oil (about 1/4 inch) in a high-sided skillet and cook the rolls 5 minutes per side until an internal temperature of 165 degrees F. Drain on paper towels for a minute before serving.

Porchetta

6 servings

One of the foods I seek out when I visit my daughter in Rome is the stuffed pork roast called porchetta. In her neighborhood, you can get it sliced at the deli counter at the back of the little neighborhood market, at sandwich shops that hand slice the meat into succulent slabs and serve it on soft buns, or even at street vendors' carts in the tourist area. This is a little more health conscious than the Italian version and relies on a simple gravy to provide extra moisture.

INGREDIENTS

3 to 4-pound boneless loin of pork

2 sprigs each fresh basil, parsley, sage, thyme and rosemary

4 tablespoons olive oil

2 cloves garlic

1 teaspoon salt

½ teaspoon cracked black pepper

GRAVY:

4 tablespoons flour

2 cups chicken stock

Salt and pepper to taste

STEPS

1. Preheat the oven to 325 degrees F.

2. Using a sharp knife, cut a 1/2-inch slice of the pork along the top or fatty side of the roast without cutting all the way through. Push this flap back and roll the roast a quarter turn then cut down along the length of the roast, again without going all the way through. Open the flap further and do another quarter turn. Depending on the size of your roast you may need to make 2 or 3 similar cuts so that you end up with a single rectangle of meat that is approximately 1/2-inch thick. Sprinkle the cut side generously with salt and pepper.

3. Place the fresh herbs, garlic and olive oil in a food processor and mix to a thick paste. Add more oil if necessary. Spread the paste evenly on top of the cut side and roll tightly back to original shape. Use kitchen twine to secure at 2-inch intervals so that the roast won't unravel during cooking.

4. Place on a rack in a shallow baking pan and roast for 2 hours or until the meat registers 175 degrees F at the thickest point. Remove the roast from the oven, tent with foil and allow to rest for 15 to 20 minutes before carving.

5. *For the gravy:* While the roast is resting, sprinkle the flour into the roasting pan and cook on the stove top until the flour is a rich brown color. Add the chicken stock and whisk until the gravy comes to a boil. Cook for another minute or two and then strain into a pan to keep warm. Remove the twine from the roast and cut into 1/4-inch slices. Serve with pan gravy.

Braciole

Makes 6

When my girls were still young I enjoyed entertaining, but the budget was pretty tight and called for careful planning. One time, I decided to serve a roast beef to our guests and estimated we'd have enough left over to provide another meal and lunches for several days. Unfortunately, one of our guests had an appetite like a fugitive from the chain gang and he didn't get up from the table until the entire roast was gone!

On the opposite side of the table, I remember showing up at a friend's house for dinner one night. There were six of us and the hostess ceremoniously set before us a steaming platter with one perfectly cooked chicken. It wasn't a big, fat roasting chicken, but a smallish, although tasty-looking, fryer. Maybe her cookbook said it could be cut into six pieces but I was one of the people who ended up with one wing!

INGREDIENTS

- **1 pork tenderloin, approx. 16 ounces**
- **1 cup breadcrumbs**
- **¼ cup olive oil**
- **¼ cup grated pecorino Romano cheese**
- **½ teaspoon oregano**
- **½ teaspoon basil**
- **Salt and pepper**
- **3 tablespoons fresh parsley, chopped**
- **1 clove garlic, minced**
- **2 hard boiled eggs, sliced**
- **2 tablespoons olive oil for frying**

STEPS

1. Cut the tenderloin into three pieces crosswise and then each piece in half lengthwise. Pound each piece carefully until it's about 1/4-inch thick.

2. In a heavy skillet, brown the breadcrumbs until they are golden. Take them off the heat and add the olive oil, cheese, spices, parsley and garlic. Top each piece of pork with the breadcrumb mixture and a few slices of egg. Roll up tightly, tucking in the sides as you go and secure the bundle with toothpicks or kitchen twine.

3. Brown the bundles in olive oil and then add them to your favorite pot of tomato sauce. Simmer for at least 1½ hours. Served with pasta, one braciole per person should be enough – unless you're having my brothers over for dinner.

Opinions on what constitutes a serving vary widely. Some sources will tell you to count on a pound and a half of spare ribs per person but only a half pound of turkey. Weight Watchers tell you a serving of meat is about the size of a deck of cards. A serving of potatoes or pasta is the size of your fist. They never met my Uncle Frank. My best advice is to know your audience. Read the recipe carefully and try to estimate how many ways you'll need to split the total. Here's a recipe for tiny bracciole made with pork tenderloin.

Spiedini

Makes 10 skewers

I have reached an age where memories from sixty years ago are more accessible and vivid than things happening in the last twenty-four hours. This recipe holds a memory of my great-grandfather, cooking tasty meat skewers over a fire in an old bucket in the backyard. Papa took an old leaky bucket and transformed it into an impromptu barbecue tool by punching holes in the bottom and putting in a small piece of screening near the bottom. He put crumpled newspaper in the bucket and covered it with the screening and then a few pieces of wood. He lit the paper from the bottom and waited for the wood to turn to embers before he rested skewers of the little rolled meat pieces over the top of the bucket. In those days I believe he used veal for the meat because it was not as expensive then and was easier to cut and pound into thin slices. My frugal mom switched the recipe to beef and that's the way we make it to this day.

INGREDIENTS

3 to 4 pounds beef eye round

3 cups breadcrumbs

Pinch oregano

Pinch basil

Salt and pepper

1 tablespoon parsley

Juice of one lemon

Olive oil

½ pound mozzarella

2 small tomatoes

STEPS

1. Freeze the eye round overnight and then allow to thaw in the refrigerator for another day. This will make it possible to cut the thinnest slices of the beef. If you have a slicing machine you can set it at 1/16th of an inch.

2. Mix all the dry ingredients into 1½ cups of the breadcrumbs. Moisten with the lemon juice and enough oil to make a paste. Lay out slices of the beef and top each with a teaspoon of the breadcrumb mixture, a sliver of mozzarella and a sliver of tomato.

3. Roll up into an oblong bundle, tucking in the sides as you go. Put onto a skewer, securing the end of the bundle. Put four or five spiedini on each skewer. Dip the completed skewers in olive oil and coat with the remaining breadcrumbs. Barbecue or broil in the oven for 2 to 3 minutes per side.

Rack of Lamb with Marmalade Sauce

2 to 4 servings

Contributed by
**Jolina Giaramita, La Tavola
Restaurant, Pittsburgh**

Jolina: Years ago when I started working for my parents as a young cook, I sought to create a dish that would really impress them. Something that would let them know I was ready to head their kitchen. It had to be a dish with a 'wow' factor that was simple enough to execute for a busy dinner service. Just roasting the lamb was not going to cut it. So, instead of roasting the lamb... I stuffed it! It is quite simple, really. Once all of your ingredients are laid out, you will be done before you know it! It is always a great centerpiece for entertaining guests, not to mention impressing your Sicilian parents!

INGREDIENTS

2 racks of lamb

**1 teaspoon, plus
1 tablespoon extra
virgin oil, divided**

1 clove garlic

2 cups baby spinach

½ onion, sliced thin

Salt and pepper

**2 tablespoons plain
breadcrumbs**

4–6 slices prosciutto

**4 slices provolone or
mozzarella cheese**

Kitchen string

Fresh rosemary or thyme

MARMALADE SAUCE:

1 teaspoon honey

1 teaspoon Dijon mustard

**2 tablespoons marmalade
(apricot or cherry)**

2 tablespoons mayonnaise

Salt and pepper

STEPS

1. Prepare the lamb for stuffing by slicing the meat away from the bone (careful not to separate from bone) and slowly cut the meat to open it up to a flat slab. Set aside.

2. Preheat the oven to 350 degrees F.

3. In a sauté pan, heat 1 teaspoon olive oil and garlic and sauté the baby spinach until wilted. Remove from heat and set aside. In another pan, heat 1 tablespoon of olive oil and sauté the onion on low heat until soft. Season onion with salt and pepper and add in the breadcrumbs. Lay out your ingredients and begin to layer onto the meat. First the prosciutto, then the cheese, then the onion and breadcrumb mixture, and finally, the spinach.

4. Carefully roll the meat toward the bone, being gentle to not lose the filling. Once the meat is rolled up, use cooking string to secure the meat so it stays in place while cooking. Season the lamb with salt, pepper and fresh rosemary or thyme. Drizzle with extra virgin olive oil and bake for 20 to 25 minutes. Let rest for 10 minutes before slicing. Serve with the marmalade sauce.

Poussin with Cornbread Stuffing

4 servings

Poussin is the French term for a very young chicken, usually only about one pound each. You can substitute Cornish game hens or just use fryers. To complete the illusion, I like to serve these with roasted baby carrots, pattypan squash and fingerling potatoes.

INGREDIENTS

FILLING:

½ **pound breakfast sausage**

3 **tablespoons butter**

1 **large onion**

1 **large Granny Smith apple, peeled, cored and chopped**

1 **cup chicken stock**

½ **teaspoon ground sage or poultry seasoning**

3 **cups cornbread stuffing mix**

½ **cup chopped pecans**

4 **poussin, 1 to 1½ pounds each, rinsed and dried thoroughly**

1 **lemon**

Salt and pepper

1 **stick butter, melted**

STEPS

1. Preheat the oven to 400 degrees F.

2. *For the filling:* Brown the sausage in a large skillet, breaking the meat into small pieces. Remove from the pan and drain the excess fat. Add the butter to the pan and cook the onion until soft. Add the apples and cook until they begin to soften. Return the sausage to the pan along with the chicken stock and use a wooden spoon to scrape the flavorful bits from the bottom of the pan. Add the cornbread stuffing mix, seasoning and pecans and toss until well mixed and moistened.

3. Rub the outside of each poussin with the lemon and season inside and out with salt and pepper. Fill each bird loosely with 1/2 cup of the stuffing and secure the legs with twine. Baste with the melted butter and roast for 20 minutes. Reduce heat to 350 degrees F and tent with foil for the next 20 minutes. Remove the foil, brush again with butter and allow to cook until the skin is crispy and the internal temperature is 170 degrees F.

Note: This recipe also works with larger chickens but you'll need to adjust cooking times accordingly.

Stuffed Turkey Breast

4 to 6 servings

A 25-pound turkey may look great as the centerpiece of your Thanksgiving feast, but it's pretty impractical for most other times of the year. This recipe uses the boneless turkey breasts that are available year-round in most supermarkets. It still looks great on the table and serving is quick and easy, with each slice a combination of both meat and stuffing.

INGREDIENTS

FILLING:

½ **pound bacon, diced**

2 **tablespoons butter**

1 **onion, diced**

1 **stalk celery**

1 **teaspoon powdered sage**

8 **cups bread cubes, toasted**

½ **cup chicken broth**

Salt and pepper

1 **to 3-pound boneless turkey breast**

Salt and pepper

STEPS

1. *For the filling:* Brown the bacon, butter, onion and celery in a high-sided skillet. Add the sage, bread cubes and chicken broth and stir until the bread has absorbed the moisture. (You can add some chicken stock if the mixture seems too dry.) Season heavily with salt and pepper and set aside to cool.

2. Preheat the oven to 400 degrees F.

3. Remove and save the skin from the turkey breast. Place the meat on a cutting board and butterfly the breast by slicing horizontally from the rib area almost to the backbone side. Spread the meat and pound slightly to create a rectangle. Season with salt and pepper.

4. Spread the stuffing on the turkey breast and roll up, starting at one rib side. Cover the rolled-up roast with the reserved skin and tie the roast with cooking twine (string) at 2-inch intervals.

5. Place on a rack in a roasting pan and cook for 30 minutes and then lower the temperature to 350 degrees F and cook for 1 hour or until it reaches an internal temperature of 165 degrees F.

6. Use the pan drippings to make gravy while the roast rests for 15 to 20 minutes.

Stuffed Pork Chops with Sweet Potato Gravy

4 servings

It seemed like every time we did another cooking special on WQED we would receive another recipe from Monica "Skippy" Narr and her sister. They were clearly recipes from someone who truly loved to cook and eat! And every time, I would try to convince Monica to come on the show and demonstrate her recipe. She always declined. "Skippy" is not with us any more but her memory lives on in the joyful and delicious recipes she shared. This one is for a decadent version of stuffed pork chops.

INGREDIENTS

2 large sweet potatoes or yams

8 tablespoons (1 stick) butter

1 cup half & half or heavy cream

Salt and pepper

Nutmeg

1 onion, diced

1 Granny Smith apple, diced

½ cup walnuts

1 cup breadcrumbs

4 thick pork chops with pockets cut into them along the sides

Personal spice dust (to season)

STEPS

1. Preheat the oven to 350 degrees F.

2. Cook sweet potatoes in their skins until fork tender. Peel then mash with 4 tablespoons of butter and the half & half or cream. Season with 1/2 teaspoon salt and a dash each of pepper and nutmeg. (Reserve 1 cup of mixture for stuffing). Place remaining mixture in a buttered 8 x 8-inch baking dish.

3. *For the filling:* Mix together 1 cup sweet potato mixture, onion, apple, walnuts, and breadcrumbs.

4. Sprinkle pork chops with your favorite personal spice dust (as simple as salt and pepper or as complex as your favorite spice mixture). Spoon stuffing inside of chops, and place atop the sweet potato mixture in the baking dish. Cover with aluminum foil and bake for 1 to 1½ hours, depending on pork chop thickness.

Mozzarella Surprise Meatloaf

6 servings

Meatloaf is one of those comfort foods that always brings me back to my childhood. You could think of it as poor man's roast beef but I think of it as an opportunity for creativity in the kitchen, with combinations of flavors that are so much more interesting. This version includes a nice, oozy surprise in the middle, with flavors from the classic Italian meatball.

INGREDIENTS

1 cup plain breadcrumbs

1 teaspoon dry oregano

2 tablespoons chopped fresh parsley (or 1 tablespoon dry)

1 egg

½ cup milk

½ cup grated pecorino Romano cheese

Salt and pepper

2 pounds chopped meat

¼ pound low moisture, part skim mozzarella

½ cup tomato sauce

STEPS

1. Preheat oven to 350 degrees F.

2. Add the breadcrumbs, spices, egg, milk and pecorino Romano cheese to a large mixing bowl. Mix and let sit for 10 minutes for the breadcrumbs to absorb the milk. Season with salt and pepper and add the chopped meat. Mix until well-combined.

3. Put half the mixture in a 9 x 5-inch loaf pan and press firmly to eliminate air pockets. Make a channel down the center of the loaf just short of each end. Cut the mozzarella into strips and press into the channel. Add the remaining meat mixture on top and press down again. Pour the sauce over the top and place in the oven. Bake for 45 minutes or until an internal temperature of 170 degrees F.

PART FIVE

SWEETS

Sure, a chocolate cookie is delicious. But it doesn't compare to a gob! (two soft chocolate cookies surrounding a pillow of pillowy white cream). We love it when there is something inside. Surprise us! Cream, custard, jelly, fondant — it's what's inside that counts. What's the most popular commercial cookie in the world? Is it the pecan sandie? No! It's the Oreo with its center of sweet cream. The flavor combinations are endless for filled sweets. More than anything else, I think that the juxtaposition of textures and flavors between inside and out is what we find intriguing. Like all the other stuffed recipes, these tend to be labor intensive because they generally have to be crafted one at a time. But the wait is worthwhile.

On March 19th the swallows return to Capistrano and Italians (especially Sicilians) celebrate the Feast of Saint Joseph. The tradition dates back to the Middle Ages during a terrible drought. The people prayed to St. Joseph for relief and in return for his intercession, they promised a great feast. The rains came and each year the people build a special altar to St. Joseph and pile it high with sweet and savory treats. Most importantly, the feast is made available to the poor who are invited to participate. Throughout Italy, each area has its own specialty for this feast, like the little jam-filled dumplings of Bologna, the deep fried zeppole of Naples or the pasta with fennel and sardines of Sicily that is served with toasted breadcrumbs instead of grated cheese.

In our house, my mother always made cream puffs called "Sfingi di San Giuseppe." At that time I didn't know the background of the tradition. I just knew that it was my father's name day and I thought Mom made them because they were my father's favorites.

Cream Puffs (Sfingi Di San Giuseppe)

Makes 24

INGREDIENTS

PASTRY:

1 cup water

8 tablespoons vegetable oil

½ teaspoon salt

1 cup flour

4 eggs

FILLING:

1 pound ricotta cheese (drained)

½ cup powdered sugar

1 teaspoon vanilla

1 tablespoon Amaretto or other liquor

¼ cup candied orange peel, chopped fine

½ cup chopped dark chocolate

STEPS

1. Preheat the oven to 450 degrees F.

2. Bring water to a boil. Add the oil and salt and then add the flour all at once. Stir until it forms a ball and comes away from the side of the pot. Remove from the heat and beat in the eggs one at a time until each is incorporated.

3. Drop by tablespoon onto a greased pan. Bake for 10 minutes, then reduce the heat to 350 degrees F and cook until golden brown. Make a slit in the side of each puff to release steam.

4. *For the filling:* Pass the ricotta through a fine mesh sieve. Beat in the powdered sugar and vanilla, and liquor, if desired. Fold in the chopped orange peel and chocolate. Fill the puffs when they are cool and dust the tops with powdered sugar.

Cannoli

Makes 12

My dear Aunt Amelia was probably my favorite of all my grandmother's sisters. She was widowed early in her marriage and left to raise her two daughters on her income as a seamstress. She specialized in zipper installation. Aunt Amelia and I also shared the challenges of living with the effects of childhood polio. But what really endeared her to all of us was the box of pastries she would bring to Sunday dinner. Inside that box were our favorite cookies as well as a number of cannoli with their sweet cream filling and crunchy crusts. There were rarely enough for us all to have our own but every bite was precious. When I got older and started to cook, I realized it would now be possible for me to make (and eat) as many cannoli as I cared to have. It stands as one of the great revelations of the power of home cooking and as a sweet reminder of Aunt Amelia.

INGREDIENTS

FILLING:

1 pound ricotta

¾ cup confectioner's sugar

1 tablespoon rum or brandy

1 teaspoon vanilla

¼ cup candied orange peels, chopped

¼ cup mini chocolate bits

SHELLS:

3 cups flour

¼ cup sugar

1 teaspoon cinnamon

¼ teaspoon salt

3 tablespoons shortening

2 eggs, well beaten

¼ cup red wine

10–20 wooden or aluminum cannoli molds

½ cup toasted pistachio nuts, finely chopped

Powdered sugar for dusting

STEPS

1. *For the filling:* Put the ricotta in a strainer over a bowl and allow to drain in the refrigerator overnight. Whisk in the confectioner's sugar, rum and vanilla. Pass the mixture through a fine sieve or a double layer of cheesecloth. Stir in the finely diced orange peels and the chocolate bits. Cover and refrigerate until ready to serve.

2. *For the shells:* Place the flour, sugar, cinnamon and salt in a large bowl. Cut in the shortening as you would to make a pie crust. Add the beaten eggs and mix well. Add the wine a tablespoon at a time until a firm dough forms. Turn the dough out onto a lightly floured board and knead until smooth. Wrap in plastic and refrigerate for 30 minutes.

3. From a piece of cardboard cut out an oval pattern 6 x 4½ inches. Heat oil in a deep saucepan or deep fryer to 360 degrees F. Roll out the dough to 1/8-inch thickness and use the pattern and a pastry cutter to form ovals from the dough. Wrap the dough loosely around the molds, brush the overlapping area with egg white and seal the edges.

4. Fry about 8 minutes, turning carefully until golden brown. Drain and cool completely before filling with ricotta cream. Sprinkle the ends with chopped pistachio and dust the tops with powdered sugar.

Lady Locks

Makes 24

We were shooting a short television documentary about the food specialties that abound in a Pittsburgh neighborhood called McKees Rocks when a local foodie led us to an unmarked doorway in a modest row house on Main Street. When we walked through the door we were in a basement bakery where four or five ladies were turning out thousands of perfect little filled cookies called Lady Locks. The outside cookie is light and crunchy and the inside is a gossamer sweet cream.

INGREDIENTS

2 sticks butter, room temperature

½ cup Crisco

1 (8-ounce) package cream cheese, room temperature

2 egg yolks

4 cups flour

FILLING:

1 cup milk

2–3 tablespoons cornstarch

1 cup Crisco

1 cup sugar

STEPS

1. Beat butter, Crisco and cream cheese together, add egg yolks and blend. Add flour, a little at a time. Refrigerate overnight. Take out half the dough. Keep what dough you›re not using in the refrigerator.

2. Preheat the oven to 350 degrees F.

3. Roll your piece of dough out in powdered sugar, rolling into a rectangle 10 x 6 inches. Cut 12 strips 1/2-inch wide and 10 inches long with a knife, then roll each strip around a clothespin which has been covered with tin foil and sprayed with non-stick. Place on ungreased cookie sheet. Repeat with remaining dough. Bake for 8 to 10 minutes. Let cool for a few minutes, then remove clothespin. Cool completely and then fill.

4. *For the filling:* Cook milk and cornstarch until thick; let cool. Beat Crisco and sugar until well blended. Add cooled cornstarch mixture. Use a piping bag to fill each cylinder.

Paczki

Makes 12

Throughout Eastern Europe there are dozens of varieties of these decadent filled doughnuts. This Polish version is often filled with plum jam or other thick preserves. The idea was to use up all the rich ingredients in the house like sugar, butter and cream before the austere regimens of the Lenten season. In the United States, Paczki day is celebrated on Fat Tuesday, the Tuesday. before Ash Wednesday. In Poland, it is celebrated on Fat Thursday, the Thursday before Ash Wednesday.

In case you would like to take some of the sting out of the caloric guilt I have included a method for baking instead of frying the doughnuts.

INGREDIENTS

DOUGH:

1½ cups flour

½ cup sugar

½ teaspoon salt

¾ cup milk

4 tablespoons butter

2 teaspoons yeast, one packet

2 egg yolks

½ teaspoon vanilla

Canola oil for frying

FINISHING:

Granulated sugar for dusting

1 (12-ounce) jar raspberry or other fruit preserves for filling

STEPS

1. In the bowl of a stand mixer, combine the flour, sugar and salt. Heat the milk in the microwave and add the butter. Let cool until thermometer measures 115-120 degrees F. Stir in the yeast and let sit for 5 minutes. Pour into the bowl with flour.

2. Add egg yolks and vanilla and mix on low until combined. Knead for 8 minutes. If the dough is too loose and sticky, add flour 1 tablespoon at a time until the dough comes together. Put the dough on a floured board and work a few turns to form a smooth ball. Cover with plastic wrap and let it rest for 10 minutes.

3. Flour the board and roll the dough out to 1/2-inch thickness. Cut out rounds with a floured 2½-inch biscuit cutter. Place the rounds on a parchment lined baking sheet. Cover with a tea towel and let rise for 45 minutes to 1 hour.

4. Heat about 1 inch of oil in a 2-quart saucepan to 325 degrees F. Push your thumb into the center of each doughnut (This will help the centers to cook through) and drop into the oil. Don't overcrowd the pan. As soon as they are brown on one side, flip them over to brown on the other. Remove with a strainer and put into a bowl with sugar. Roll them around to coat with sugar. Put on a rack to cook slightly.

5. Fit a pastry bag with a long tube and fill doughnuts with your preserves. Insert the pastry tube into the side of each doughnut and fill with a generous amount of preserves. These are best when served fresh and warm.

ALTERNATIVE BAKING METHOD:

1. Preheat the oven to 375 degrees F.

2. Place the paczki in the oven for 10 minutes until deep golden brown. As soon as they come out of the oven, baste the top and sides of each doughnut with melted butter and bounce them around in a plastic bag to coat with sugar. Fill as above.

Vienna Tarts

Makes 32

Each year on the last Sunday in December before Christmas, we invite friends from our church or work and other acquaintances to join us for refreshments and singing, and tell them that if they want to bring something, a small plate of cookies would be fine. We purposely schedule the event in the early evening and encourage people to bring children (their own or others'), older people and any instruments they wouldn't be too shy to try playing along with the singing. Well, nobody seems to listen. Oh, not about the children or the instruments. In those areas, the more the merrier. It's the cookies! The table is soon groaning with a magnificent assortment of treats from simple cutouts to glorious concoctions with nuts and colored sprinkles, lady locks and gingerbread figures to snickerdoodles and giant oatmeal raisins.

INGREDIENTS

4 ounces dried apricots

1 (12-ounce) jar apricot preserves

2 sticks butter or margarine, softened

2 (3-ounce) packages cream cheese, softened

2 cups flour

1 egg, beaten

Walnuts, chopped

Sugar and cinnamon

STEPS

1. Chop dried apricots and add to the apricot preserves. Cook in a saucepan until preserves are thickened.

2. Mix butter and cream cheese. Add flour and form into two balls. Refrigerate 4 hours or overnight.

3. Preheat the oven to 350 degrees F.

4. Divide each ball into 4 smaller balls. Roll each ball out onto a floured surface to about a 10-inch diameter circle. Cut the circle into 4 quarters. Place a tablespoon of thickened apricot preserves at the base of each section and roll up toward center, tucking in sides slightly as you go. Repeat with the remaining balls of dough to create 32 cookies.

5. Place the rolled tarts on a greased cookie sheet or on parchment paper. Brush with beaten egg and sprinkle with chopped walnuts or sugar and cinnamon. Bake about 15 minutes until golden brown.

After we've all sung ourselves hoarse with "The 12 Days of Christmas" and eaten our way through the cookie wonderland, people begin to load up bags and plates of leftover cookies to take home. Like the loaves and fishes, the little treats seem to have multiplied so that it's possible for everyone to leave with more cookies than they brought! It's one of the true mysteries of the season. The nicest part of the whole event is the chance to actually do something with family and friends rather than just watch all the Christmas specials on television.

If you want to make a plate of cookies that will be welcome at any party, or if you just want to treat visitors at your house during the holidays, I suggest the simple and delicate cookies my mother always made for us – Vienna Tarts. She used to fill them with different flavors of jam but we all liked the apricot best.

Apple Dumplings

Makes 6

I came to apple dumplings late in life. We often had apple pie at home and baked apples were a fall treat. But this stuffed recipe is a magical combination of the two with overtones of caramel apple and cinnamon. I still like to make these in the fall when local apples like Empire and Rome Beauty are available at the farmers' market.

INGREDIENTS

FILLING:

1 cup brown sugar

6 tablespoons butter

½ cup walnuts

¼ teaspoon cinnamon

Dash of salt

6 Rome Beauty Apples, peeled and cored

6 pie crusts (8 to 9 inches square)

SAUCE:

½ cup honey

½ cup brown sugar

½ cup water

¼ teaspoon cinnamon

2 tablespoons butter

STEPS

1. Preheat the oven to 350 degrees F.

2. *For the filling:* Put the brown sugar, butter, walnuts, cinnamon and salt in a food processor and pulse until the nuts are chopped and the butter is cut into small clumps.

3. Place each apple on a square of pie dough and fill the center with the mixture. Bring up the sides of the pie crust and fold around the apple to cover completely. Pinch the edges to seal.

4. *For the sauce:* Combine the honey, brown sugar, water and cinnamon in a saucepan. Stir until the sugar is dissolved and cook over medium heat for 2 minutes without stirring. Remove from the heat and add the butter.

5. Place the dumplings about 1 inch apart in a baking dish and spoon the sauce over them. Bake for 40 to 45 minutes, basting every 10 minutes with the sauce. Serve with vanilla ice cream and syrup from the pan.

Plum Crostada

It seems to me that people used to eat a lot more plums than they do today. Depending on the season we ate big red plums or small, dark purple Italian plums. When ripe, plums are sweet and delicious with an appealing firm flesh. For this recipe I use the large red plums of the fall, but depending on the season, you could use the smaller varieties or even fresh apricots. You can roll the sweet crust directly on a baking sheet or on a piece of baking parchment if you like. Just make sure that the baking sheet has a lip because some liquid from the filling may seep out of the crostada during baking.

INGREDIENTS

DOUGH:

2 cups all-purpose flour

¼ cup sugar

½ teaspoon salt

1½ sticks of butter

6 to 8 tablespoons cold water

FILLING:

3 cups ripe plums, pitted and sliced ⅛-inch thick

½ cup firmly packed brown sugar

1 tablespoon orange juice

½–1 teaspoon freshly grated orange zest

STEPS

1. Preheat the oven to 400 degrees F.

2. Combine flour, sugar and salt in bowl; cut in butter until mixture resembles coarse crumbs. Mix in water with fork until flour is just moistened. Press or roll pastry into 14-inch circle on ungreased baking sheet.

3. Arrange plums in pinwheel fashion on pastry. In a bowl, stir together brown sugar, orange juice and orange zest and spread evenly over plums. Fold the edges of the pastry over the plums to create a 2-inch border. Bake for 25 minutes or until pastry is golden brown. Sprinkle with powdered sugar just before serving, if desired.

French Crepes With Nutella

Makes 6

A crepe without filling looks like a failure. It just lies there, limp and unfulfilled. We don't think much of them here in America, but take a trip to Paris and crepes are available in store windows and from street vendors everywhere. They pour the batter onto a heated metal dome and smooth it down to an even layer with a rake-like stick. When it is brown on the bottom they deftly flip it with another stick to brown the other side. They add a dollop of Nutella® and fold it into quarters before wrapping in some waxed paper and handing it to you to eat as you stroll the Boulevard St. Germaine on your way to the Musee Cluny.

I have recently become a convert to the joys of self-rising flour. It makes for fluffy biscuits, pancakes and even scones without additional leavening.

INGREDIENTS

1 egg

1 teaspoon sugar

1 teaspoon vanilla

1 cup self-rising flour

1 cup milk, or more

FILLINGS:
(choose one or more)

Nutella

Peanut butter

Jelly or preserves

Cream cheese

STEPS

1. Beat the egg with the sugar and vanilla. Add the flour and then enough milk to form a very thin crepe batter. Allow the batter to rest for 30 minutes. Check the consistency again and adjust with more milk or flour as needed.

2. *To assemble:* heat an 8- or 10-inch non-stick pan and coat with a little butter. Pour in 1/4 cup of the batter and swirl the pan to make a very thin crepe. Let the crepe set until well browned on the bottom and dry on the top. Turn the crepe and cook for a few seconds more. Turn again and smear the top with a tablespoon of the filling of your choice. Fold the crepe into half and then quarters, enclosing the filling. Serve immediately.

Hand Pies

Makes 12

This is an easy treat to make in the fall when apples are plentiful (and economical). Be careful to use an apple variety that will stay firm through the cooking process. I like Rome Beauties, Emperors, Granny Smith and even Golden Delicious. These also make terrific additions to any lunchbox.

INGREDIENTS

DOUGH:

2½ cups all-purpose flour

½ teaspoon salt

1 stick unsalted butter, chilled and cut into small pats

½ cup ice water

FILLING:

2–3 large apples, peeled, cored and diced

Juice of ½ lemon

½ cup sugar

½ teaspoon cinnamon

Pinch of salt

1 tablespoon instant tapioca

1 egg, beaten (for egg wash)

STEPS

1. Put the flour and salt in the bowl of a food processor and pulse to mix. Add the pats of cold butter and pulse until the mixture looks like coarse meal. Add the water a tablespoon at a time until a dough forms and cleans the sides of the bowl. Remove and wrap in plastic wrap. Chill for at least 30 minutes or overnight.

2. Preheat the oven to 400 degrees F.

3. *For the filling:* mix the apples, lemon juice, sugar, cinnamon, salt and tapioca in a bowl.

4. Divide the dough in half and roll out on a floured board. Use a biscuit cutter to form 3-inch rounds. Place a tablespoon or so of the filling on each circle. Fold over and crimp the edges with a fork. Place on a parchment lined baking sheet and cut a few slits in each little pie to let steam escape.

5. Brush with the egg wash and bake for 20 to 30 minutes or until the outsides are dark golden brown and the filling is bubbly. Remove to a rack to cool.

Note: There is nothing to keep you from adding some raisins and chopped toasted walnuts or pecans to the filling. But the apple is the star of this show.

Eclairs

Makes 12

When my grandmother's sister, Amelia, would come to our house for Sunday dinner, she always brought a big box of pastries from the pasticceria near her house. It was a mouthwatering collection of pignolia cookies, 7-layer cookies, biscotti, cannoli and on some occasions the exotic eclair! We begged my mother to try and make these at home so that we didn't have to split the one eclair in the box into three tiny pieces. Mom was successful and I never had to share an eclair again.

INGREDIENTS

PASTRY:

1 cup water

8 tablespoons vegetable oil

½ teaspoon salt

1 cup flour

4 eggs

FILLING:

1 cup milk

1 (4 ½-ounce) box vanilla instant pudding mix

2 cups heavy cream, whipped to soft peaks

CHOCOLATE TOPPING:

8 ounces dark chocolate, chopped into small pieces

4 ounces heavy cream, warmed

3 tablespoons butter, melted

2 ounces light corn syrup

Pinch of salt

STEPS

1. Preheat the oven to 450 degrees F.

2. Bring water to a boil. Add the oil and salt and then add the flour all at once. Stir until it forms a ball and comes away from the side of the pot. Remove from the heat and beat in the eggs one at a time until each in incorporated. Pipe the dough onto a parchment-lined cookie sheet in the shape of 4-inch logs.

3. Bake for 10 minutes, then reduce the heat to 350 degrees F and cook until golden brown. Make a slit in the side of each log to release steam.

4. *For the filling:* Whisk milk and instant pudding and let sit till thickened, about 5 minutes. Fold into whipped heavy cream. Put into a pastry bag with a wide opening and fill the shells.

5. *For the chocolate topping:* Place the chopped chocolate in the top of a double boiler. Warm the cream and butter in a bowl in the microwave until the butter is melted. Pour into the melting chocolate and stir in the corn syrup. Stir until the mixture is completely smooth. Remove from heat and let cool slightly before pouring over the filled eclairs.

Cream-Filled Chocolate Cupcakes

Makes 12

Growing up in the 1950s, we were the first generation of American youth to be bombarded by television advertisements for all the things we didn't even know we needed. Lots of them were food: Chef Boyardee, Swanson's Pot Pies, Maltex, and Hostess Cakes. Hostess made a variety of sweet snacks like Devil Dogs, Coffee Cakes and, my favorite, the Hostess Cupcake with the creamy white filling and little curlicue frosting on the top. Now that I have this recipe, I can finally have my fill.

INGREDIENTS

CUPCAKES:

½ cup all-purpose flour

⅓ cup cocoa powder (I use Hershey's Special Dark)

½ teaspoon baking powder

¼ teaspoon baking soda

¼ teaspoon salt

2 eggs

¾ cup canola oil

½ cup sugar

FILLING:

6 tablespoons butter

1½ cups confectioner's sugar

¾ cup marshmallow fluff

2 tablespoons heavy cream

ICING:

¼ cup heavy cream

4 ounces chocolate bits or chopped chocolate

1 tablespoon butter

STEPS

1. Preheat the oven to 350 degrees F. Line a muffin tin with paper baking cups.

2. Mix the dry ingredients together in a bowl. To the bowl of a mixer, add the eggs, oil and sugar and mix until light and creamy. Gradually add the dry ingredients until the batter is smooth. Do not over-mix. Fill each baking cup about halfway and bake for 15 to 20 minutes until a toothpick comes out clean. Remove the cakes from the tin and let cool completely on a rack.

3. *For the filling:* Cream the butter and sugar. Mix in the marshmallow fluff and enough of the heavy cream to make an icing that you can pipe. Place the filling in a pastry bag with a long plain tip. Insert the tip in the top of a cupcake and squeeze in filling until you feel the cake start to expand. Repeat with the other cupcakes.

4. *For the icing:* heat the cream in a small saucepan just until bubbles begin to form around the edges. Take off the heat and add the chocolate. Stir until completely smooth, then add the butter and stir.

5. Dip each cupcake into the chocolate ganache icing. Let cool for a minute and then use the filling to form the squiggle across the center.

Cuccidati

Makes about 6 dozen

There is something uniquely appealing about "lost" food. The fond memory of a youthful roadtrip can elevate a mundane bowl of chowder at a roadside restaurant into the best seafood you have ever eaten. And if there is little likelihood that you will ever travel that particular route again, the memory will go unchallenged. Is the macaroni and cheese ever as creamy, the pie pastry ever as flaky, the pickles ever as crunchy as the ones we remember? Newspapers and magazines often carry columns where readers dredge up food memories in the hopes of finding compatible recipes to duplicate those dishes. In my experience it is probably an exercise in futility. But then...

Two years ago I was reminiscing with my sisters, Pauline and Patricia, about the filled cookies that were as much a part of the holiday atmosphere at our house as the bubble lights on the tree. We had a wonderful time remembering my mother and grandmother working as a team to grind the dates, raisins

INGREDIENTS

FILLING:

1½ pounds figs

1 pound dates

½ pound raisins

1 orange, with skin

½ cup sugar

½ cup brown sugar

1 cup hazelnuts, toasted

½ teaspoon cinnamon

¼ bottle liqueur (Frangelica, B&B, Cointreau, Amaretto)

¼ cup honey

DOUGH:

7 eggs

½ teaspoon vanilla

½ cup milk

1½ cups sugar

¾ cup shortening (Crisco)

8 cups flour

2 tablespoons baking powder

Dash of salt

1 egg yolk, beaten with 1 teaspoon water

STEPS

1. Preheat the oven to 375 degrees F.

2. *For the filling:* Grind figs, dates, raisins and orange together. Mix with sugars, hazelnuts, cinnamon, liqueur and honey. Set aside for a few hours or overnight to let flavors blend.

3. *For the dough:* Beat eggs well. Add vanilla and milk. Beat sugar and shortening together and gradually add to eggs. Continue to beat. Mix 1 cup flour with baking powder and salt. Add it to the wet ingredients and continue adding flour until a soft dough forms. Knead gently 5 or 6 times.

4. Divide into 4 parts. Use a rolling pin to roll out to 1/8-inch thickness. Cut into 4-inch circles. Moisten the edges with a little egg wash. Take about 3 tablespoons of the fruit mixture and shape into a 3-inch-long log about as thick as your pinky finger. Place on the center of the circle, fold over and crimp the edges and then form into a crescent shape. Place on parchment paper on a cookie sheet. Brush with egg wash and sprinkle with colored non-pareils. Bake for about 20 minutes or until lightly browned.

and oranges, lacing the mixture with toasted nuts and some kind of spirits. Then they would make the fragile cookie dough that wrapped around the filling in a crescent shape and finish each off with a shiny egg wash and a sprinkling of multi-colored non-pareils. The results were like individual fruitcakes and formidable enough to anchor any holiday meal.

Thirty years slipped away since the last batch came out of my mother's oven and the recipe receded too far in her memory to be recaptured. We didn't even know the name of the cookies so that we could research other formulas and piece together our own version. Then, my friend George McHale gave me a book called Bruculinu, America: Remembrances of Sicilian-American Brooklyn, Told in Stories and Recipes, by actor Vincent Sciavelli. There they were: the filled cookies called cucidata! I made a few minor adjustments and have to admit that the recreation has proven to be every bit as delicious as the original — but still not as sweet as the memory.

Gobs

Makes 12

These tasty treats are nothing more than giant, homemade Oreo cookies. Here in Western Pennsylvania they are called gobs or "Whoopie Pies."
This title supposedly derives from the reaction of young children to finding one of these confections in their lunch box. Once you have the technique down you can experiment with other flavors of batter and filling. Think Pumpkin Spice, Strawberries and Cream or even Chocolate Peanut Butter.

INGREDIENTS

BATTER:

½ cup unsweetened cocoa

2 cups all-purpose flour

1½ teaspoons baking soda

½ teaspoon baking powder

½ teaspoon salt

½ cup vegetable shortening (we used Crisco)

1 cup sugar

1 egg

1 cup whole milk

2 teaspoons vanilla extract

FILLING:

½ of a 16-ounce container marshmallow fluff

1 cup confectioner's sugar

½ cup vegetable shortening

¼ teaspoon vanilla extract

1 tablespoon milk (approx.)

STEPS

1. Preheat the oven to 450 degrees F. Line two cookie sheets with parchment paper.

2. In a medium bowl, combine cocoa, flour, baking soda, baking powder and salt. Stir to mix. Set aside. In the bowl of a stand mixer with the paddle attachment, cream together the shortening and sugar. Add egg, milk, and vanilla extract and mix well. Slowly add dry mixture to the mixing bowl with the wet mixture and mix well.

3. Using a medium (1½-ounce) scoop, place scoops of the batter onto the prepared cookie sheets (about 12 per sheet). Bake one cookie sheet at a time for 6 to 7 minutes. With a spatula, remove immediately to cool on a wire cooling rack.

4. *For the filling:* Combine the marshmallow fluff, confectioner's sugar, shortening and vanilla extract in the bowl of a stand mixer and mix well. Add milk as necessary to get to a soft consistency. Place a dollop of the filling in the center of the flat side of one cake. Place a matching piece of cake against the filling and push to spread the filling evenly between the two halves.

Stuffed Strawberries

As a special treat, we used to go to a landmark restaurant in Brooklyn called Junior's for a slab of their world famous cheesecake. I always ordered the strawberry version because I love the combination of the fruit flavor with the tangy sweetness of the cheesecake. Making an entire cheesecake is quite a production but you can achieve a similar flavor profile with these colorful and delicious bitefulls.

INGREDIENTS

1 pound strawberries, washed, dried and hulled

¼ pound cream cheese, softened

¼ cup confectioner's sugar

½ teaspoon vanilla

STEPS

1. Use your hulling tool or the tip of a paring knife to ream out a small cavity on the top of the strawberry.

2. Mix the cream cheese with the confectioner's sugar and vanilla until smooth and creamy. Spoon into a piping bag or a plastic bag with one of the tips cut. Spoon the filling into the bag and pipe a small amount into the top of each strawberry.

3. If you want to complete the cheesecake connection you can sprinkle some graham cracker crumbs on top. Or you can create a nice color contrast by topping the cream with a single blueberry.

Nut Rolls

Makes 6

Contributed by
Carol and Holly Rosborough

Holly: This nut roll recipe was given to my mother (Carol) from a neighbor many years ago; we don't know too much about it except that it's a Polish recipe. As is probably with most folks, since I grew up with this, it's the one I prefer most for nut rolls. The dough results in a beautiful flaky crust, and the filling isn't too sweet. This nut roll was always on the Christmas cookie tray, along with chocolate chip cookies, date nut balls, thumbprints, Russian tea cakes and others. Mum would keep these in the freezer that we kept out in the garage, and while we kids could pilfer a "few" Christmas cookies every now and then (you know, taste-testing), we couldn't make a whole nut roll disappear!

INGREDIENTS

DOUGH:

8 cups flour

1 teaspoon salt

4 tablespoons baking powder

1 pound butter

1 (12-ounce) can evaporated milk

1 large yeast block (in grocery refrigerator section)

1 teaspoon granulated sugar, plus more for rolling out the dough and sprinkling on top

4 large eggs

NUT MIXTURE:

2 pounds ground walnuts (get out the processor!)

1 cup sugar (approx.)

1 (12-ounce) can evaporated milk

1 teaspoon vanilla

STEPS

1. Sift flour with salt and baking powder in a very large bowl. Cut in butter; mix as with a pie crust. (I've used a processor for this step and it works really well.)

2. Heat canned milk to lukewarm and add crumbled yeast and sugar. Let this mixture stand while you beat eggs until foamy. Add milk/yeast mixture and eggs to flour mixture. Mix until dough comes off hands. Let dough cool in refrigerator for 4 hours or overnight...or let rise for 1 hour and then fill with nut mixture and bake right away – your choice.

3. *For the nut mixture:* Combine walnuts, sugar, milk and vanilla in a heavy saucepan; cook over low heat for 15 to 20 minutes. Let cool completely. (It's a good idea to make the night before, along with the dough.) Also, I sometimes add a little regular milk to the mixture, as I find that it's usually too thick to spread.

4. Preheat the oven to 400 degrees F.

5. Divide dough into 6 balls if you're making larger nut rolls. Sprinkle the board with some sugar and roll out like pie dough. Spread on the nut mixture and carefully roll up the dough. Tuck in dough at the ends and place seam side down on a baking sheet. Sprinkle the tops of the rolls with some sugar and bake until brown, about 30 minutes. (If you're making smaller rolls, adjust baking time to about 15 to 20 minutes.)

It wasn't a Christmas without these nut rolls. When I make these today, the aroma takes me back to years ago, watching my mum make these. She used a hand-crank grinder to grind the nuts; today I use the food processor. It's best to grind them as finely as possible for a smooth filling. And be sure to roll these in sugar, not flour; it won't make them too sweet, but results in a better nut roll. They take a bit of practice but are worth making. I hope this recipe becomes a part of your Christmas and other holiday baking.

ACKNOWLEDGMENTS

ABOUT THE AUTHOR

Acknowledgments

First and foremost, I would like to thank the generous folks who were willing to share their family stories and recipes with us for this book. We know how precious these are and hope you are as encouraged as we are that these recipes will now continue to spread as memories in other families.

Sevil Bostanci Aktas
Dr. James Baran
Yu Ling Cheng Behr
Alberto Benzaquen
Joseph Certo
Dave and Aimee D'Anoia
Maryanne Fello
Joseph Fennimore
Carolyn Fronapel
Jolina Giaramita
Pat Joyce
Luella Ouano McClernan
Julie Mueller
Monica "Skippy" Narr
Carol Rosborough
Arthi Subramaniam
Karen Tracy
Mary Ann Williams

Next, I have to recognize our amazing and tireless photographer, Laura Petrilla, who dragged tons of equipment, dishware, backgrounds and tableware to my house for seven separate days of cooking, photographing, feasting and fun. Your art is as delicious as the food itself!

I also want to thank my daughter, Maryann Kranis, who donated her artistic talents for the whimsical drawings that punctuate these pages with such style. I guess those art lessons at the Carnegie finally paid off.

For more than twenty-five years I have accomplished nothing without the encouragement, inspiration, and assistance of my dear wife and partner, Laura. This book is no exception. She was the first person to hear the idea for the book and has guided its development to this day.

Finally, I am grateful to the staff at St. Lynn's Press for guiding this novice through the rigors of cookbook production: Paul Kelly who embraced this project after only one bite of calzone; Cathy Dees, my patient and gentle editor; and Holly Rosborough, our designer, who even helped with the dishes.

About the Author

For the past twenty-five years, Chris Fennimore has been a popular figure on Pittsburgh's WQED public television. An Emmy and James Beard Award winner, he has produced and hosted a long-running series of cooking programs (called "QED Cooks" in Pittsburgh and "America's Home Cooking" when episodes air around the U.S.). Unlike other cooking formats, these shows – and the resulting 100-plus public television cookbooks used in membership drives – invited the viewers to send their family treasures and share their kitchen wisdom.

For *Stuffed*, he has included some of the best "stuffed" recipes from those home cooks. The rest of the recipes are his, collected over the years from family and friends and made his own – predominantly ethnic comfort foods with long and well-loved traditions. His previous cookbook was *Simple Pleasures* (St. Lynn's Press, 2017).

OTHER BOOKS FROM ST. LYNN'S PRESS

www.stlynnspress.com

Dutch Treats

by William Woys Weaver

208 pages • Hardback
ISBN: 978-1943366040

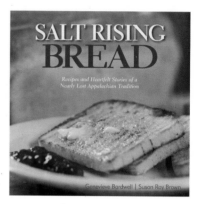

Salt Rising Bread

by Genevieve Bardwell and Susan Ray Brown

160 pages • Hardback
ISBN: 978-1943366033

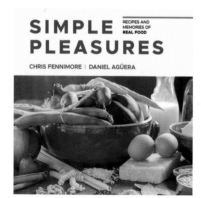

Simple Pleasures

by Chris Fennimore and Daniel Agüera

192 pages • Hardback
ISBN: 978-1943366323

A Taste for Herbs

by Sue Goetz

192 pages • Hardback
ISBN: 978-1943366385